CO-AYP-701

By The Editors of
CONSUMER GUIDE®

FAVORITE BRAND NAME RECIPES

APPETIZERS
DIPS & SNACKS

Fawcett Crest • New York

KILL$$$FAV
Favorite Brand Name Recipes
copyright page

A Fawcett Crest Book
Published by Ballantine Books
Copyright © 1982 by Publications International, Ltd.

Published in the United States by Ballantine Books, a division of Random House, Inc., New York, and in Canada by Random House of Canada, Limited, Toronto, Canada.

Library of Congress Catalog Card Number: 82-80954

ISBN: 0-449-24568-3

This edition published by arrangement with Publications International, Ltd.

Manufactured in the United States of America

First Ballantine Books Edition: October 1982

Cover Design: Anthony Russo
Cover Photography: David Spindel

Contents

Introduction

Favorite brand name recipes—classics so good that they have stood the test of time, as well as the popular new recipes that satisfy even the choosiest cooks—these are exactly the ones the Editors of CONSUMER GUIDE® have chosen for *APPETIZERS, DIPS & SNACKS*.

Clipping recipes from food labels and packages is a unique American cooking tradition. Now for the first time, we have compiled an extensive selection of brand name favorites from a single culinary category.

For ease of use, the book is divided into four sections—"Appetizers," "Quickie Appetizers," "Dips" and "Party Snacks"—to enable you to locate just the right recipe for any occasion. Whenever possible, recipes of a similar type, such as sausage appetizers, are also grouped together.

For the convenience of our readers, we have included an address directory of the manufacturers of all brand name food products listed in the book (see Acknowledgments). Any questions or comments about the recipes should be directed to the individual manufacturers for prompt attention.

CONSUMER GUIDE® wishes to thank all of the participating food companies for their excellent contributions. By reprinting these recipes—exactly as they appeared on their original labels or packages—CONSUMER GUIDE® is offering a handy collection of proven recipes, not endorsing particular brand name products.

Appetizers

ANTIPASTO

1 small head cauliflower,
    separated into flowerets
1 green pepper, cut into strips
1 large carrot, cut into sticks
4 stalks celery, sliced
2 tomatoes, cut into eighths
1 jar (8 ounces) HEINZ Spiced
    Onions, drained
2 cloves garlic, minced
½ pound small button mushrooms
1 cup olive or salad oil
1¾ cups HEINZ Apple Cider or
    Wine Vinegar
⅓ cup granulated sugar
2 tablespoons HEINZ Mild Mustard
2 teaspoons salt
1 teaspoon oregano leaves
Anchovies
Olives

Combine first 6 ingredients in large
bowl. Sauté garlic and mushrooms
in oil until mushrooms are tender.
Add vinegar and next 4 ingredients;
pour over vegetables. Cover; chill
overnight, stirring occasionally.
Drain well; serve on lettuce-lined
platter. Garnish with anchovies,
ripe or stuffed olives.
        Makes 10-12 servings (8 cups)

MARINATED VEGETABLE HORS D'OEUVRES

1 small cauliflower, broken into flowerets
2 green peppers, cut into ½-inch strips
½ pound small mushroom caps
5¼ ounce can black pitted olives, drained
4½ ounce jar white cocktail onions, drained
¾ cup olive oil
¼ cup salad oil
¼ cup MINUTE MAID® 100% Pure Lemon Juice
1¼ cups white wine vinegar
¼ cup sugar
2 teaspoons salt
¾ teaspoon ground pepper
1 clove garlic, minced

Mix vegetables together in a shallow dish. Bring remaining ingredients to a boil, cook five minutes and pour over vegetables. Cover and marinate for 24 hours in the refrigerator. Drain and serve with toothpicks.

BERTOLLI® STUFFED ARTICHOKES

4 medium artichokes
Juice of 1 lemon
1 rib celery, thinly sliced
½ red pepper, cut into strips
¼ cup finely chopped onion
1 tablespoon BERTOLLI® Olive Oil
1 cup cooked peas
2 tablespoons walnut pieces
¼ cup BERTOLLI® Olive Oil
1 tablespoon BERTOLLI® Red Wine Vinegar
1 teaspoon sugar
Dash each salt and pepper

Cut stem and 1-inch top from artichokes; cut tips off leaves. Rub artichokes with lemon juice; heat to boiling in 2-inches water in saucepan. Reduce heat; simmer covered until tender, about 30 minutes. Drain; cool. Separate top leaves; remove chokes with spoon. Sauté celery, pepper and onion in 1 tablespoon oil in skillet 4 minutes. Stir in peas and walnuts. Mix remaining ingredients; stir into vegetables. Spoon vegetables into center of artichokes. Serve hot or refrigerate and serve cold.

Makes 4 servings

DEVILED HAM STUFFED CUCUMBERS

2 medium cucumbers
1 can (4½ ounces) UNDERWOOD®
   Deviled Ham
1 hard-cooked egg, coarsely
   chopped
1 tablespoon finely chopped onion
1 tablespoon finely chopped sour
   pickle
1 teaspoon prepared mustard

Cut cucumbers in half lengthwise
and scoop out seeds. In a bowl,
mix together deviled ham, chopped
egg, onion, pickle and mustard.
Spoon mixture into cucumber
shells. Chill. When ready to serve,
cut cucumber diagonally into 1
inch pieces.

*Makes about 2 dozen
hors d'oeuvres*

CHEESEY CELERY SNACK

Combine: ½ lb. grated CHEEZ-
OLA,® ¼ cup finely chopped ripe
olives, 2 tablespoons chopped
green pepper, dash of garlic
powder, ½ cup safflower
mayonnaise. Stuff celery stalks or
serve on crackers or bread.

DANNON® YOGURT

YOGURT STUFFED CELERY

1 bunch celery
2 cups DANNON® Plain Yogurt
½ cup mashed blue cheese
½ cup finely chopped chives
1 Tbsp. brandy
Salt to taste

Wash celery and cut into 2″ pieces. Combine yogurt, blue cheese, chives and brandy. Chill until hardened to spreading consistency. Fill celery pieces and serve cold.

Makes filling for approximately 20 pieces

VARIATION:

Put 2 cups of DANNON® Plain Yogurt through a cheese cloth. Drain for 24 hours. Mix "yogurt cheese" remaining in cloth with blue cheese, chives, brandy and salt. Fill celery pieces and serve cold.

Makes filling for approximately 12 pieces

CAVIAR-STUFFED CELERY

1 bunch celery
1 pkg. (8 oz.) cream cheese, softened
2 Tbsp. milk
1 Tbsp. chopped chives
2 Tbsp. chopped parsley
2 Tbsp. (1 oz.) ROMANOFF® Caviar*
Additional caviar for garnish

Trim and wash celery stalks. Cut to make sixteen 2½ inch pieces. Mix cheese with milk until smooth. Stir in chives, parsley and caviar. Spoon onto celery pieces. Cover. Chill. Just before serving, garnish with additional caviar.

Makes 16 pieces

*ROMANOFF® Red Lumpfish or Salmon Caviar suggested.

BACON-STUFFED MUSHROOMS

1 lb. fresh mushrooms
2 Tbsp. chopped onion

2 Tbsp. butter
1 slice bread, torn into small
  pieces
1 cup (4 oz.) shredded Cheddar
  cheese
1 can (3 oz.) OSCAR MAYER Real
  Bacon Bits

Remove stems from mushrooms
and set aside caps; chop stems.
Cook onions and chopped
mushroom stems in butter until
tender; add bread pieces. Remove
from heat; stir in bacon bits and
cheese. Mound filling in caps;
place in shallow baking pan. Bake
in 400°F oven 15 min. until cheese
is melted. Serve warm.

Makes 15-20 appetizers

STUFFED MUSHROOMS

1 pound medium mushrooms
  (about 18)
¼ cup butter or margarine, melted
¼ cup green onions, finely
  chopped
¼ cup water, white wine or sherry
1 cup PEPPERIDGE FARM® Herb
  Seasoned Stuffing

continued

continued

Wash mushrooms and remove stems. Dip caps in melted butter and place upside down in a shallow baking pan. Finely chop ¼ cup of the mushroom stems and sauté with green onions in remaining butter, adding more butter if necessary. Add water or wine. Lightly stir in stuffing. Spoon mixture into mushroom caps. Bake at 350°F. until hot, about 10 minutes.

Makes about 18 hors d'oeuvres

CHEEZ-IT® STUFFED MUSHROOMS

1 cup fine CHEEZ-IT® Crackers crumbs (about half a 6¼ ounce package)
½ teaspoon salt
¹⁄₁₆ teaspoon pepper
1 pound large mushrooms
⅓ cup minced onion
⅓ cup minced celery
⅓ cup butter
3 tablespoons minced parsley

Prepare crumbs, a little at a time, in an electric blender or crush with rolling pin between two pieces of waxed paper. Mix with salt and pepper and set aside. Clean mushrooms and save stems for later use in soups or sauces. Sauté onion and celery in butter over moderate heat until soft; do not brown. Remove from heat; stir in parsley and crumbs. Stuff into mushroom caps. Place caps, stuffed side up, in shallow pan. Pour enough water in bottom of pan to come up about one-quarter the depth of the mushroom caps. Bake in very hot oven (450°F.) for 25 to 30 minutes, or until mushrooms are tender but not mushy. *Yield: 4 servings*

STUFFED EGGS
(Uova Torino)

10 hardboiled eggs, shelled
½ cup mayonnaise
1 teaspoon prepared hot mustard
Dash TABASCO® Sauce
1 tablespoon LIQUORE GALLIANO®
Red caviar
Green pepper strips

Halve eggs lengthwise and remove yolks. Mash or sieve yolks, mix in mayonnaise, mustard, TABASCO® and LIQUORE GALLIANO®. Blend until very smooth. Press yolk mixture through pastry bag into egg white halves. Garnish with red caviar and pepper strips. Chill.
Makes 20

DEVILISH EGGS*

6 hard-cooked eggs, halved
3 tablespoons mayonnaise
1 tablespoon LEA & PERRINS
  Worcestershire Sauce
½ teaspoon onion powder
Dash TABASCO® Sauce
2 tablespoons finely chopped nuts

Remove yolks from whites, being careful not to break egg whites; set whites aside. In a small bowl mash egg yolks. Add mayonnaise, LEA & PERRINS, onion powder and TABASCO®; mix well. Mound mixture into egg whites using a spoon or pastry bag fitted with a tube. Garnish with chopped nuts.
  Yield: 12 stuffed egg halves

*May be prepared in advance of serving.

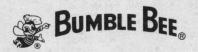

TUNA STUFFED TOMATOES
(Low Calorie)

1 can (6½ oz.) BUMBLE BEE®
  Chunk Light Tuna in Water
½ cup chopped celery

⅓ cup imitation or low calorie
  mayonnaise
¼ cup chopped parsley
2 tablespoons minced green onion
¼ teaspoon black pepper
36 cherry tomatoes
Parsley sprigs for garnish

Drain tuna. Combine tuna, celery,
mayonnaise, chopped parsley,
green onion and pepper. Cut tops
off tomatoes and scoop out seeds;
turn upside down to drain. Fill with
tuna salad. Serve chilled on
parsley lined plate.
Makes 36 appetizers
21 calories per appetizer

YOGURT ANCHOVY EGG SPREAD

6 hard boiled eggs, chopped
2 cups DANNON® Plain Yogurt
2 Tbsp. anchovy paste
¼ cup chopped scallions
12 olives, chopped
1 small dill pickle, chopped
Pepper to taste

In a bowl, mix eggs, yogurt,
anchovy paste and scallions, olives
and pickles. Season with pepper.
Chill until ready to serve. Garnish
with chopped chives. Serve spread
on brown bread or crackers.

EGG-AND-CAVIAR SPREAD

8 hard-cooked eggs, chopped
¼ cup softened butter
2 tsp. prepared mustard
½ cup (4 oz.) ROMANOFF®
  Caviar*
3 Tbsp. lemon juice
1½ Tbsp. Worcestershire
4 Tbsp. mayonnaise for garnish
Rye bread slices

Combine eggs, butter, mustard and two-thirds (about five tablespoons) of the caviar with lemon juice and Worcestershire, blending well. Spoon into serving dish; cover and keep cold at least one hour. Just before serving, spread mayonnaise over top. Garnish with remaining caviar. Provide servers, so guest may spread on rye bread slices.

Enough for 8

*ROMANOFF® Red Salmon Caviar suggested.

LIVERWURST SMORREBROD

1 can (4¾ ounces) UNDERWOOD®
  Liverwurst Spread
2 tablespoons mayonnaise
12 slices party rye bread

24 slices cherry tomato
12 slices cucumber
2 tablespoons chopped scallion

In a bowl, mix liverwurst spread
and mayonnaise. Spread on party
rye slices. Top with slices of cherry
tomato, cucumber and chopped
scallion.   *Makes 12 snacks*

THE FOOLER

2 cans KING OSCAR Sardines
1 medium onion, grated
½ apple, peeled and grated
2 Tbsp. vinegar
½ tsp. sugar
2 hard-cooked eggs, chopped

Combine all ingredients and mix
thoroughly. Let stand in
refrigerator until chilled. Use as
hors d'oeuvre or in sandwiches.

BERTOLLI®
MARINATED SHRIMP

1½ pounds cooked shrimp in
    shells
½ cup BERTOLLI® Olive Oil
¼ cup BERTOLLI® Red Wine
    Vinegar
2 tablespoons BERTOLLI®
    Spaghetti Sauce

continued

continued

2 tablespoons horseradish mustard
½ cup celery, minced
½ cup green onions, minced
½ cup drained capers
1 clove garlic, minced
1 ½ teaspoons paprika
½ teaspoon salt
Dash cayenne pepper
Shredded lettuce
Lemon wedges

Peel shrimp, leaving tails on. Mix remaining ingredients, except lettuce and lemon in medium bowl; stir in shrimp. Refrigerate covered 12 hours, stirring 2 or 3 times. Spoon onto lettuce-lined plate; garnish with lemon.

Makes 6-8 servings

MARINATED SHRIMP

1 can (4 ½ ounces) LOUISIANA BRAND Shrimp
½ cup any favorite oil and vinegar type dressing

Drain shrimp. Cover with dressing. Marinate in the refrigerator 2 hours or longer.

HOW TO SERVE THEM

1. As an appetizer before dinner . . .on shredded lettuce . . . atop tomato, cucumber, or avocado

slices . . . with grapefruit sections,
a little marinade drizzled over.

2. As party food with picks and
plenty of crackers . . . on the plate
with assorted fresh vegetable
relishes . . . dotted on pizza
snacks . . . broiled on bread rounds
or crackers *under* dabs of melting
cheese, especially blue . . . as
"dunks" for cheese fondue right
along *with* the bread cubes.

3. Tossed in mixed green salad . . .
chef's salad with cheese, ham, or
chicken . . . potato salad.

4. For family snacks . . . refrigerated. They keep *and* keep.

BRAUNSCHWEIGER RING

1 package (3 oz.) lemon gelatin
¾ cup boiling water
1 can (8 oz.) tomato sauce
1 tablespoon vinegar
½ teaspoon salt
1 package (1 lb.) OSCAR MAYER
  Braunschweiger Liver Sausage

Add gelatin to boiling water; stir
until dissolved. Mix in tomato
sauce, vinegar and salt. Chill until
slightly thickened. Gradually add
to liver sausage and blend well.
Pour into lightly oiled 1 quart mold.

continued

continued

Chill thoroughly. Unmold on serving plate. Garnish with hard-boiled egg (finely chop egg white and sieve egg yolk). Serve as a spread with crackers.

(PARTY) TUNA MOLD

2 6½ oz. cans tuna
1 8 oz. package cream cheese, softened
2 Tbsp. minced onion
2 Tbsp. chopped parsley
1½ Tbsp. BALTIMORE SPICE OLD BAY Seasoning
1½ Tbsp. catsup
½ Tbsp. prepared horseradish

Drain tuna. Mix together remaining ingredients. Add tuna and beat until well blended. Pack into 4 cup mold or small bowl; chill thoroughly. To serve, unmold onto a plate, garnish with parsley and/or olives and serve with crackers.

CHERRY HAM CANAPÉS

1 package (3 oz.) cream cheese, softened
1 tablespoon orange juice
½ teaspoon grated orange peel
2 tablespoons finely chopped walnuts

16 slices party rye bread
4 slices (4 oz.) thinly sliced ham
16 Northwest fresh sweet
  cherries, pitted

Combine cream cheese, orange juice and peel, and walnuts. Spread about ½ tablespoon of the cheese mixture on each slice of bread. Cut each slice of ham into 4 triangles; place one triangle on top of cream cheese mixture. Top each canapé with a pitted cherry, secured with a toothpick.

Makes 16 canapés
Recipe from Northwest Cherry Growers

KASHA TABBOULI

1 cup cooked WOLFF'S® Kasha*
  (buckwheat groats)
  (whole, coarse, or medium)
⅓ cup chopped green onions
About 15 fresh mint leaves,
  chopped
¼ cup chopped parsley
1 large tomato, seeded and
  chopped
Salt to taste
1 Tbsp. lemon juice
Red wine vinegar & oil dressing
Romaine leaves

Tabbouli is best prepared with kasha that has been cooked in

continued

continued

chicken broth. Combine all ingredients, using sufficient salad dressing to moisten kasha (about 3-4 Tbsp.). Chill for at least 2 hours before serving. Place tabbouli in center of plate, surround it with romaine leaves to be used as "scoops" to eat this tangy appetizer. (If available, a food processor speeds preparation).

> *Serves 4-5 as hors d'oeuvre or*
> *2-3 as salad course*

*To cook WOLFF'S® Kasha:
1 cup uncooked WOLFF'S® Kasha
1 egg, slightly beaten
2 cups boiling liquid (water is O.K., but broth, consomme or bouillon is better)
1 tsp. salt**
¼ tsp. pepper
2 Tbsp. butter or margarine (optional)

In two-quart saucepan or skillet, combine kasha, egg, and seasonings. Stir constantly over medium heat for about two minutes or until the egg is "set" and each grain is separate and dry. Add boiling liquid, cover pan tightly, and cook gently over low heat for 15 minutes or until kasha grains are tender. If desired, stir in butter or margarine.

> *Makes about 3 cups*

**Use less if broth is highly seasoned.

BACON CHEESE NIBBLES

**3 tablespoons FRENCH'S®
Sesame Seed
1 envelope (5 servings) FRENCH'S®
Idaho Mashed Potato Granules
1 egg, slightly beaten
¼ cup mayonnaise
½ cup shredded Cheddar cheese
5 to 6 slices bacon, crisply cooked
and crumbled
FRENCH'S® Paprika**

Spread sesame seed in shallow
pan. Toast in 350° oven 5 to 8
minutes, stirring occasionally, until
golden brown. Prepare mashed
potatoes following directions on
package, except decrease water to
⅔ cup. (Potatoes will be very stiff.)
Stir in egg, mayonnaise, cheese,
and the crumbled bacon. Shape
into small balls, using a rounded
teaspoonful for each. Roll in
toasted sesame seed; sprinkle with
paprika. Arrange on greased
baking sheet. Bake in 400° oven 10

continued

continued

to 15 minutes, until golden brown.
Serve hot as hors d'oeuvres.

4 to 5 dozen

Crunchy Ham Nibbles: Omit bacon
and cheese. Stir in 1 cup very
finely diced ham, ¼ cup each very
finely diced celery and pickle.
Shape, roll in sesame seed, and
bake as directed above.

OLIVE LOAF
CORNUCOPIA

Cut slices of ECKRICH® Olive
Loaf in half. Spread with Mustard
Spread.* Roll to form small
cornucopias. Fill opening with
additional Mustard Spread. Place
cornucopias on slices of buttered
cocktail rye bread.

Makes 16 servings

*MUSTARD SPREAD

¼ cup butter, softened
6 ounces cream cheese, softened
3 Tbsp. mayonnaise
2½ tsp. prepared mustard
1 tsp. sugar

In electric mixer, cream butter and
cheese until light and fluffy. Blend
in remaining ingredients.

Makes one cup

CHEERY CHEESE SPREAD

½ cup THE CHRISTIAN
   BROTHERS® Ruby Port
¼ cup cream
½ tsp. paprika
1 tsp. grated onion
¾ lb. sharp cheddar cheese,
   diced
¼ lb. blue cheese, crumbled

Combine ingredients in blender;
whirl until smooth. Pack into small
crocks or containers to store in
refrigerator or give as gifts. *2 cups*

DANISH CHIPWICH

1 ⅓ cups crab meat (flaked fine)
¼ cup mayonnaise
¼ cup finely chopped pickled
   onions
Hard cooked egg
Green pepper
Olives
Large JAYS Potato Chips

Method: Stir mayonnaise and
onions into crab meat. Spread on
large crisp Potato Chips and
garnish with olive slices or green
pepper strips and hard cooked egg
slices.

ARNOLD SORENSIN SPRATT SPREAD

2 cans of ARNOLD SORENSIN
   Spratts
8 oz. of cream cheese, softened

Just drain the oil from the Spratts
and blend the two ingredients
together in a food processor or
with a fork. Refrigerate for a few
hours. Serve with melba toast,
crackers or on bread of your
choice.

CHEESY CORN SPREAD

12 oz. (3 cups) shredded sharp
   Cheddar cheese
½ cup dairy sour cream
½ cup salad dressing or
   mayonnaise
¼ cup finely chopped onion
½ teaspoon salt
12-oz. can GREEN GIANT®
   MEXICORN® Golden Whole
   Kernel Corn with Sweet Peppers,
   drained

Bring cheese to room temperature. In large bowl, crumble cheese with fork or blend with mixer to form small bits. Mix in remaining ingredients, except corn, until well blended. Stir in corn. Cover; chill several hours or overnight. Can be stored in the refrigerator up to 1 week. Serve with raw vegetables or crackers. *3½ cups*

High Altitude—Above 3500 Feet: No change.

NUTRITIONAL INFORMATION PER SERVING

SERVING SIZE:		PERCENT U.S. RDA	
1 Tablespoon		PER SERVING	
Calories	40	Protein	3
Protein	2 g	Vitamin A	2
Carbohydrate	2 g	Vitamin C	*
Fat	3 g	Thiamine	*
Sodium	95 mg	Riboflavin	2
Potassium	15 mg	Niacin	*
		Calcium	5
		Iron	*

*Contains less than 2% of the U.S. RDA of this nutrient.

AYRSHIRE CHEDDAR SPREAD

½ lb. Cheddar cheese (or other medium-sharp, firm cheese)
3 oz. cream cheese, softened
3 tablespoons JOHNNIE WALKER Red
⅛ teaspoon salt
⅛ teaspoon pepper
2 teaspoons chopped chives

continued

continued

Grate cheese and mix with other
ingredients until well combined.
Refrigerate several hours to
mellow. Serve with tray of assorted
crackers, rye-crisp and dark bread,
as a cocktail accompaniment.

About 1 ½ cups

Note: Mixture spreads more easily
at room temperature.

SMOKY CHEESE SPREAD

4 oz. Cheddar cheese, grated
1 8 oz. pkg. cream cheese
1 3 oz. wedge Roquefort cheese
(optional)
1 teaspoon WRIGHT'S Natural
Hickory Liquid Smoke
Chopped parsley or chopped
pecans

Bring cheeses to room
temperature. Mix all ingredients,
except parsley or pecans, in
electric mixer or food processor.
Shape into ball if desired, roll in
parsley or pecans. Chill. Serve with
assorted crackers.

HAM AND CHEESE-CHIP PINWHEEL

3-ounce package cream cheese
2 tablespoons mayonnaise

½ teaspoon prepared mustard
2 teaspoons horseradish
⅓ cup chopped stuffed olives
¼ teaspoon paprika
1 teaspoon grated onion
⅔ cup finely crushed JAYS
  Potato Chips
6 thin slices boiled ham

Combine and blend all ingredients
except ham. Spread mixture on
ham slices. Roll each edge
lengthwise and fasten with small
wooden picks. Chill. Cut rolled
ham crosswise into thin slices.
Serve with potato chips.

COTTAGE CHEESE NUT RING

2 pounds cottage cheese
½ cup PLANTERS® Dry
  Roasted Mixed Nuts
1 teaspoon curry powder

Combine cottage cheese,
PLANTERS® Dry Roasted Mixed
Nuts and curry powder; beat until
thoroughly blended. Place cheese
mixture in a greased 9-inch ring
mold. Chill until firm (about 2
hours). Unmold and serve with
sliced fresh fruit.

Makes 6 servings

FRUIT CHEESE LOG

½ cup DEL MONTE Dried Apricots
1 cup water
1 lb. Monterey Jack cheese,
    shredded
1 pkg. (8 oz.) cream cheese,
    softened
⅓ cup milk*
1 tsp. poppy seed
½ tsp. seasoned salt
⅓ cup DEL MONTE Golden
    Seedless Raisins
¼ cup pitted dates, snipped
¾ cup chopped walnuts
Crackers

Soak apricots in water two hours;
drain and chop. Blend cheeses.
Add milk, poppy seed and salt; mix
well. Fold in fruit; mix well. Turn
out on foil; shape into log-type roll.
Wrap securely in foil; chill until
firm. Roll in nuts before serving.
Serve with crackers.

1 log (approximately 2 lbs.)

*VARIATION:

Substitute ⅓ cup sherry for milk.

SMOKY PIMIENTO CHEESE BALL

One 8-oz. container WISPRIDE
 Hickory Smoked Cold Pack
 Cheese Food, softened
One 8-oz. package cream cheese,
 softened
¼ cup bacon crumbs (4 strips,
 cooked and crumbled)
1 tablespoon chopped pimiento
1 teaspoon Worcestershire sauce
½ teaspoon lemon juice
½ cup finely chopped pecans

In small bowl, combine WISPRIDE
and cream cheese; beat until
smooth and creamy. Add bacon,
pimiento, Worcestershire sauce
and lemon juice; mix well. Chill in
refrigerator until pliable (about 1
hour). With spatula or wooden
spoon, shape into a ball. Roll in
pecans.   *Makes one cheese ball*

CHIP CHEESE BALLS

3-ounce package cream cheese
½ cup grated raw carrot
½ cup finely crushed JAYS
 Potato Chips
Chopped parsley

continued

continued

Soften cream cheese and mix with
carrot and potato chips. Shape into
balls about an inch in diameter.
Roll in parsley. Chill and serve.

ALMOND CHEESE PINECONE

**2 packages (8 ounces *each*) cream
cheese, softened**
**2 jars (5 ounces *each*) pasteurized
process cheese spread with
pimiento**
½ pound blue cheese, crumbled
¼ cup minced green onion
½ teaspoon Worcestershire sauce
**2 cups BLUE DIAMOND®
Blanched Whole Almonds,
toasted**
Pine sprigs for garnish
Crackers

In large bowl with mixer at medium
speed, beat cream cheese, cheese
spread with pimiento and blue
cheese until smooth. With spoon,
stir in green onions and
Worcestershire sauce. Cover and
refrigerate about one hour. On
work surface, with hands, shape
cheese mixture into shape of large

pinecone. Arrange on wooden board. Beginning at narrow end of cone, carefully press almonds about ¼ inch deep into cheese mixture in rows, making sure that pointed end of each almond extends at a slight angle. Continue pressing almonds into cheese mixture in rows, with rows slightly overlapping, until all cheese is covered. Garnish pinecone with pine sprigs. Serve with crackers.

Makes about 25 servings

"PHILLY" CHEESE BELL

1 8-oz. pkg. CRACKER BARREL
  Brand Sharp Cheddar Flavor
  Cold Pack Cheese Food
1 8-oz. pkg. PHILADELPHIA
  BRAND Cream Cheese
PARKAY Margarine
2 teaspoons chopped pimiento
2 teaspoons chopped green pepper
2 teaspoons chopped onion
1 teaspoon Worcestershire sauce
½ teaspoon lemon juice

Combine cold pack cheese food, softened cream cheese and 2 tablespoons margarine; mix until well blended. Add remaining ingredients; mix well. Mold into bell shapes, using the cold pack container coated with margarine or

continued

lined with plastic wrap. Chill until
firm; unmold. Garnish with
chopped parsley and pimiento
strips, if desired.   *2 bells*

**IMPORTED
SWISS CHEESE**

COCKTAIL PARTY BALL

**1 pound shredded FINLANDIA
  Swiss
¼ pound Roquefort or Blue
  cheese, crumbled
1 package (8 ounces) cream
  cheese
1 tablespoon grated onion
2 teaspoons Worcestershire sauce
Dash cayenne pepper
½ cup chopped toasted pecans
½ cup finely chopped parsley**

Bring cheeses to room
temperature. Place in electric
mixer and blend well. Add onion,
Worcestershire sauce and cayenne
pepper. Shape into ball, wrap in
waxed paper or plastic wrap. Chill
several hours. Just before serving
combine pecans and parsley. Roll
ball in mixture. Serve with
crackers.   *Makes 8 to 10 servings*

LIVER SPREAD

1 package (3 oz.) cream cheese
1 tablespoon melted butter
1 jar (3½ oz.) GERBER® Strained
  Beef Liver
1 jar (3½ oz.) GERBER® Strained
  Chicken
1 teaspoon wine vinegar
½ teaspoon onion powder
¼ teaspoon ground mace
¼ teaspoon celery salt
⅛ teaspoon powdered basil leaves
⅛ teaspoon ground allspice
¼ teaspoon salt

Soften cream cheese with melted
butter. Add other ingredients and
blend well. Pack into small
containers. Cover and chill well
before serving.

Yield: Approximately 1 cup

CAVIAR "PIE"

6 hard-cooked eggs, chopped
3 Tbsp. mayonnaise
1 large sweet onion, finely chopped
  (1½ cups)
1 pkg. (8 oz.) cream cheese,
  softened
⅔ cup sour cream
7 Tbsp. (3½ oz.) ROMANOFF®
  Caviar*

continued

continued

Lemon wedges and parsley sprigs for garnish

Grease bottom and side of eight-inch springform pan. In a bowl, combine eggs and mayonnaise until well blended. Spread in bottom of pan to make an even layer. Sprinkle with onion. Combine cream cheese and sour cream; beat until smooth. By the spoonful, drop onto onion. With a wet table knife, spread gently to smooth. Cover. Chill three hours or overnight. At party time, top with a layer of caviar, distributing it to the edges of the pan. Run knife around sides of pan; loosen and lift off sides. Arrange lemon wedges in open pinwheel. Fill center with parsley sprigs. Serve with small pieces of pumpernickel bread.

Makes 10 to 12 servings

*ROMANOFF® Black Lumpfish or Whitefish Caviar suggested.

CHOPPED GOOSE OR CHICKEN LIVERS, MADE WITH STOCK BRANDY

Two eggs
Two onions
Two tablespoons butter
Two tablespoons chopped parsley

**One lb. chicken or goose livers
One oz. STOCK Brandy**

Drop livers into boiling seasoned
water and simmer until barely
done. Drain and cool. Hard boil the
two eggs, chop up and add. Chop
coarsely onions and sauté in
butter. Blend ingredients to fine
paste, season to taste and add
parsley and STOCK Brandy.

Serves four-six

PICNIC PÂTÉ

¼ cup butter
1½ lb. chicken livers
1 tsp. garlic salt
1 small onion, finely chopped
¾ cup THE CHRISTIAN
   BROTHERS® Riesling
1 Tbsp. Worcestershire sauce
2 hard-cooked eggs
4 drops TABASCO® Sauce
½ cup soft butter

Sauté livers, garlic salt, and onion
in ¼ cup butter for 5 minutes; add
wine and Worcestershire sauce;
simmer 5 minutes longer. Cool,
then whirl smooth in blender or
food processor with eggs. Blend in
TABASCO® and butter. Turn into
serving dish; cover and chill
overnight. *4 cups*

NATURALLY NUTTY PÂTÉ
(Low Sodium/Low Calorie)

⅓ cup uncooked brown rice
Boiling water
2 tablespoons FLEISCHMANN'S®
   Unsalted Margarine
2 cups sliced fresh mushrooms
1 cup grated zucchini
½ cup chopped onion
½ teaspoon crushed fresh garlic
1 egg
1¾ cups ground PLANTERS® Dry
   Roasted Unsalted Mixed Nuts
½ cup minced fresh parsley
¼ cup wheat germ
1 teaspoon sage
1 teaspoon basil
½ teaspoon thyme
½ teaspoon tarragon
⅛ teaspoon ground black pepper

Prepare rice in boiling water
according to package directions
eliminating salt.

Melt FLEISCHMANN'S® Unsalted
Margarine in a large skillet over
medium heat. Add mushrooms,
zucchini, onion and garlic; sauté
until tender but not browned. Puree
sautéed vegetables in blender or
food processor; transfer to a
mixing bowl. Place prepared rice
and egg in blender or processor
and blend until smooth. Add to

vegetable mixture with remaining ingredients. Mix thoroughly.
Spread into a greased 9 × 5 × 3-inch loaf pan. Bake at 375°F. for 25 to 30 minutes, or until golden around edges. Cool 30 minutes. Loosen edges with knife. Remove and cool on wire rack. Wrap and refrigerate until ready to serve.

Makes 1 loaf (9 × 5 × 2-inches)

Per serving (¼ inch slice): 50 calories, 4 mg. sodium

CHAMPIGNON CHICKEN PÂTÉ

- 1 can (5 ounces) SWANSON Chunk Chicken
- 1 can (about 2 ounces) mushrooms, drained and chopped
- 2 tablespoons mayonnaise
- 2 tablespoons finely chopped onion
- 1 tablespoon finely chopped parsley
- 2 teaspoons Worcestershire

Combine ingredients; chill. Serve on crackers. *Makes about 1 cup*

CHICKEN LIVER PÂTÉ

½ pound butter (2 sticks)
1 small yellow onion, thinly sliced
1 teaspoon curry powder
1 teaspoon salt
⅛ teaspoon paprika
Pepper
1 pound chicken livers
2 tablespoons JACQUIN'S Brandy

Melt half the butter (1 stick) in a heavy skillet. Add the onion and cook over low heat until onion is soft but not brown, about 10 minutes. With a slotted spoon, remove onion and put in blender jar. Stir curry powder, salt, paprika and a dash of pepper into the butter. Add chicken livers, a single layer at a time, and brown lightly on both sides. Remove from skillet and set aside. Add remaining butter (1 stick) to skillet, stirring as it melts to dissolve any glaze. Add brandy. Pour part of the butter into the blender jar with the onion, add a few of the livers, and blend until smooth. Gradually add remaining livers and butter, blending until smooth. (If you don't have a blender, the ingredients can be pushed through a sieve, but it's difficult and the pâté will be less smooth.) Pack the mixture into a

3-cup mold or loaf pan that has been rinsed in cold water. Chill until firm, about 2 or 3 hours. To serve, unmold on a platter and surround with crisp crackers.

PEANUT CHICKEN PICK-ME-UPS
(Low Sodium)

2½ cups ground cooked chicken
½ cup grated carrots
½ cup minced fresh parsley
½ cup finely chopped onion
¾ cup low-sodium mayonnaise
1½ cups ground PLANTERS® Dry Roasted Unsalted Peanuts
¼ cup FLEISCHMANN'S® Unsalted Margarine, melted

Toss together chicken, carrots, parsley and onion. Add mayonnaise; mix well. Roll into 1-inch balls. Roll each ball in PLANTERS® Dry Roasted Unsalted Peanuts. Dip one side of ball in FLEISCHMANN'S® Unsalted Margarine and place on ungreased baking sheets, margarine side up.

Bake at 400°F. for 15 minutes, or until golden. Cool 5 minutes before serving.   *Makes 36 1-inch pieces*

Per piece: 95 calories, 8 mg. sodium

TERIYAKI TIDBITS

14 COOKIN' GOOD Chicken Wings (about 3 lbs.)

Marinade:
1 cup teriyaki sauce
½ cup molasses
½ cup lemon or lime juice
¼ cup honey
1 teaspoon of garlic powder or
    1 clove fresh garlic crushed
¼ cup instant onions minced
1 cup vegetable oil
1 cup white wine
1 teaspoon paprika
Dipping sauce*

Disjoint wings, reserve tips for stock. In a large glass bowl, combine marinade ingredients. Add wing pieces and marinate at least four hours (preferably overnight).

Conventional oven instructions: Preheat oven to 400 degrees. Drain marinade and reserve for basting and sauce recipe. Place wing pieces in a single layer in a shallow baking dish. Roast 35-45 minutes, basting often with marinade, until crisp and brown.

Microwave instructions: Same as above except use a microwave baking dish. Microwave 12-15 minutes. Baste and stir pieces often. Crisp under browning unit or conventional broiler.

Conventional oven: bake at 400 degrees; 35-40 minutes

Microwave oven: 12-15 minutes, full power, 650 watts

*DIPPING SAUCE

2 teaspoons of cornstarch
1 cup of Marinade

Blend marinade and cornstarch together in a saucepan (without heat). Stirring constantly, bring the mixture to a boil over a medium heat until thick and bubbly. Serve this sauce with the Teriyaki Tidbits.

ZING WINGS

2½ pounds chicken wings
6 tablespoons DURKEE RedHot! Sauce
¼ cup butter or margarine, melted

Split chicken wings at each joint and discard tips; pat dry. Deep fry at 400° (high) for 12 minutes or until crispy. Remove and drain well. (Can also be baked on a rack in a 400° oven for 25 minutes.) Combine hot sauce and butter. Dip chicken wings in sauce.

Makes 6 to 8 appetizer servings

CURRIED ALMOND CHICKEN BALLS

½ cup BLUE DIAMOND® Chopped
  Natural Almonds, toasted
1 can (6½ ounces) boned chicken
1 package (3 ounces) cream
  cheese, softened
2 tablespoons chutney, chopped
1 teaspoon curry powder
Salt and pepper
Minced parsley

Finely chop almonds; set aside. In
small bowl, mix together chicken
and cream cheese, breaking up any
large chunks of chicken. Add
chutney, curry powder and
almonds; mix until well-blended;
salt and pepper to taste. Chill until
mixture is firm, about one hour.
Shape into 1-inch balls and roll in
minced parsley. Chill until ready to
serve.   *Makes about 24 (1-inch) balls*

CHICKEN VERONIQUE APPETIZERS

¾ pound cooked chicken breast,
  in ¾-inch cubes
2 tablespoons sweet French
  dressing
¾ pound Thompson seedless
  green grapes

1 package (3 oz.) cream cheese,
  softened
2 tablespoons orange juice
  concentrate
3 tablespoons sour cream
⅛ teaspoon bottled hot pepper
  sauce

Toss warm chicken in French
dressing; refrigerate 2 hours. Drain
well. On frilled toothpicks skewer 1
grape, 1 piece chicken and 1 more
grape. Arrange on platter. Beat
cream cheese until fluffy; beat in
orange juice concentrate, sour
cream and hot pepper sauce. Serve
with skewered chicken and grapes.
Makes 45 to 50 appetizers

*Favorite recipe from California Table Grape
Commission*

HOT ORIENTAL CHICKEN WING APPETIZERS

1 package (27 oz.) BANQUET® Heat
  and Serve Frozen Fully Cooked
  Fried Chicken Wing Portions
¼ cup soy sauce
¼ teaspoon cayenne pepper

continued

1. Place frozen chicken wing portions on cookie sheet.

2. Combine soy sauce and cayenne. Brush over chicken wing portions.

3. Bake in 375°F oven for 25 minutes. Serve hot.

Makes about 25 appetizers

OYSTERS ROCKEFELLER

Rock salt
¾ cup butter (1½ sticks)
3 tablespoons minced green onion
3 tablespoons minced parsley
½ cup bread crumbs
1½ cups chopped raw spinach
2 tablespoons PERNOD
1 teaspoon celery powder
2 teaspoons lemon juice
¼ teaspoon cayenne
24 bacon pieces (1 inch)
24 oysters on the half shell

Preheat oven to 425°F. Fill 6 pie plates (8 inch) with rock salt. Place oysters in shell on rock salt. Heat ¼ cup butter in heavy skillet until foaming; add minced onion and cook slowly until soft. Stir in parsley, bread crumbs, spinach, PERNOD, celery powder, lemon juice, and cayenne. Add remaining butter and mix thoroughly. Spoon mixture onto oysters by ½ teaspoonfuls, distributing evenly. Top each oyster with bacon piece. Place pans in oven and bake 8-10 minutes or until bacon is crisp-tender. Remove from oven and serve directly from pans (rock salt keeps oyster shells from tipping).

To serve canapes without shells or forks: Remove oysters from shells and place on crisp toast rounds, or in individual, oven-proof butter crocks; process as directed above.

Makes 24

OYSTERS BROCHETTE

1 can (8-oz.) HIGH SEA Oysters
6 slices of bacon
1 box round toothpicks

Drain can of oysters, discarding liquid. Cut bacon into smaller slices, sufficient to just wrap whole oysters, skewering with toothpicks. Place under broiler with a medium flame (about 350°) until bacon is cooked. Serve as hors d'oeuvre.

BAKED CLAMS ITALIANO

1 (10½ ounce) can minced clams
2 tablespoons olive oil
1 tablespoon grated onion
1 tablespoon minced parsley
⅛ teaspoon oregano
¼ cup plus 2 tablespoons
   crumbled HI HO® Crackers
1 teaspoon garlic salt
2 tablespoons grated Parmesan
   cheese

Drain clams and reserve 3 tablespoons broth. Heat olive oil in small frying pan. Sauté onion, parsley, oregano and ¼ cup crumbled crackers for 2 minutes, or until onion is golden. Remove from heat and mix with clams, 3 tablespoons broth, and garlic salt. Spoon into a dozen clam or aluminum shells. Sprinkle lightly with a mixture made of 2 tablespoons Parmesan cheese and 2 tablespoons cracker crumbs. On baking sheet, bake in 375°F. oven for 25 minutes, or until crusty on top.   *Yield: 6 servings*

BLUE CHEESE FONDUE

**4-ounce package TREASURE
   CAVE® Blue Cheese, crumbled**

½ cup dry white wine
8 ounces cream cheese, cubed
8 ounces Monterey Jack cheese,
   cubed
1 tablespoon kirsch (cherry brandy)

Heat wine and cream cheese,
stirring, until cheese melts. Add
Monterey Jack cheese, a little at a
time, stirring constantly. Blend in
blue cheese. When smooth, add
kirsch. Serve with dippers of
French bread, fresh fruit or
vegetables.   *Yield: 5 cups*

EASY DANISH CHEESE FONDUE

1½ cups dry white wine, or
   1 can (12 ounce) beer
1 clove garlic
4 cups shredded Danish Cheese*
   (combine 2 varieties)
2 Tbsp. cornstarch
1 Tbsp. brandy or akvavit
Dash of white pepper and nutmeg
¼ teaspoon baking soda

Pour wine or beer into a 2-quart
saucepan. Add garlic. Heat gently
until bubbles start to rise. Discard
garlic. Toss cheese with
cornstarch. Add the cheese by
thirds to saucepan, stirring gently
until all cheese is melted. Add

continued

continued

brandy and spices. Just before serving, stir in baking soda.

Makes four to six servings

Along with chunks of French bread, offer fresh mushrooms, celery chunks, partly cooked zucchini, broccoli or asparagus, apple wedges, bites of cooked chicken, ham or shrimp for dipping into the savory cheese fondue.

*Mild Danish Cheeses: Tybo, Danbo, Samsoe, Svenbo, Creamy Havarti (Havarti Mild) or Danish Fontina
*Full Flavored Danish Cheeses: Esrom or Havarti

Favorite recipe from Denmark Cheese Association

SWISS FONDUE

1 Tbsp. flour
1½ cups VIRGINIA DARE White Cooking Wine
Half clove garlic
¾ lb. grated Swiss Cheese
Dash of pepper
Loaf of French bread

Stir flour vigorously into about ¼ cup cold VIRGINIA DARE White Cooking Wine; then add to remainder of wine in a fondue cooker or double boiler which has been rubbed with a cut clove of garlic. Heat to just below boiling. Slowly add cheese, stirring constantly. Continue stirring to a smooth consistency and add pepper to taste. Using long handled forks, spear bite-size pieces of French bread and dip into the fondue coating the bread chunk completely. If the fondue becomes too thick through prolonged cooking, it may be thinned with the addition of a little more cooking wine.

Yield: 4 servings

CHEESE 'N MUSHROOM BALLS

4 ounce package TREASURE CAVE® Blue Cheese, crumbled
Shortening for frying
3 cups fresh bread crumbs*
2½ ounce jar mushrooms, drained and chopped
2 tablespoons chopped green onion
½ teaspoon savory
¼ teaspoon pepper
2 eggs, slightly beaten

Heat shortening to 350°F. Combine cheese, 2 cups crumbs, mushrooms, onion, savory and pepper. Fold in eggs. Let stand 10

continued

continued

minutes. Shape into balls, using rounded teaspoon for each. Roll in remaining crumbs. Deep-fat fry about 1½ minutes or until golden brown.

Yield: About 2½ dozen

*To make bread crumbs, put day-old bread in blender or rub bread with spoon through strainer.

Tip: The balls may be frozen before frying. When ready to serve, deep-fat fry 5 minutes.

DEEPFRIED DANISH CAMEMBERT CHEESE

**Danish Camembert Cheese
  (fresh or canned)**
Flour
Eggs
Bread crumbs
Oil

The cheese must be cold. Cut Camembert into small wedges. Lightly coat wedges in flour. Dip each wedge in slightly beaten eggs and coat in fine bread crumbs, then refrigerate. You can prepare the Camembert cheese several hours before frying. Fry cheese until golden in 1½ inches very hot salad oil about 1½ minutes; drain briefly on paper towels. Serve hot with toast and your favorite jam.

Favorite recipe from Denmark Cheese Association

DOWN HOME SAUSAGE AND CHEESE PIE

1 unbaked deep dish pie shell (9")
¾ lb. HILLSHIRE FARM® Smoked Sausage, chopped
2 eggs, beaten
1 cup evaporated milk
1 tsp. Worcestershire sauce
1 cup shredded Swiss cheese
¼ cup shredded cheddar cheese
½ cup chopped onion

Preheat oven to 400°. Prick bottom and sides of prepared pie crust with fork. Bake 8 minutes. Remove from oven and reduce heat to 350°. Sprinkle ½ of sausage over partially baked crust. Combine remaining ingredients (except sausage) and pour into pie shell. Sprinkle with remaining sausage. Bake at 350° for 45–50 minutes or until set. Allow to cool 10 minutes before serving.

MICROWAVE:

Place unbaked pie crust in a 9" glass (or ceramic) pie or quiche dish. Prick bottom and sides of

continued

continued

crust with fork. Brush top edge of crust with a little Worcestershire sauce. Microwave, uncovered, HIGH 4–5 minutes or until dry and opaque. Sprinkle crust with cheeses and onion and top with sausage. Pour milk into a glass bowl and microwave, uncovered, HIGH 2 minutes. Beat eggs and 1 tsp. Worcestershire sauce together and carefully whisk in the hot milk. Pour into shell. Microwave, uncovered, MEDIUM 15–18 minutes or HIGH 9–11 minutes, rotating the dish every three minutes. Custard should be slightly set in the center when done. Allow to stand 10 minutes before serving.

Yield: 6 regular servings or 16 snacks

MINI SWISS QUICHES

1 11 oz. pkg. piecrust mix
4 slices bacon, diced
½ cup chopped green onion
3 large eggs
½ tsp. salt
⅛ tsp. each pepper and nutmeg
⅔ cup THE CHRISTIAN BROTHERS® Chablis or Chenin Blanc
1½ cups shredded Swiss cheese, tossed with 1 Tbsp. flour

Prepare piecrust mix according to package directions. Roll out pastry, half at a time, to about $\frac{1}{16}$ inch thick; cut into 3 inch rounds and line muffin cups. Cook bacon until crisp; drain. Reserve 1 Tbsp. drippings. Cook onion in bacon drippings until soft. Beat eggs; mix in seasonings, wine, onion and bacon. Divide cheese mixture among lined pans and spoon egg mixture into each. Bake at 450 degrees, 10 minutes. Reduce temperature to 350 degrees and continue baking about 12 minutes until quiches are puffed and golden brown. Cool on a rack. *16 quiches*

MINI-QUICHES

1 can (8 oz.) refrigerated
  butterflake dinner rolls
1 pkg. (8 oz.) OSCAR MAYER Ham
  and Cheese Spread
2 eggs
2 green onions with tops, chopped

Separate dinner rolls into twelve pieces. Divide each piece into three sections. Press dough sections in 1¾-inch diameter tart or muffin cups, stretching dough slightly to form shell. Combine cheese spread, eggs and onion; mix well. Divide mixture evenly among shells. Bake in 375°F oven

continued

continued
for 15 min. or until golden brown.
Freeze extras; reheat on baking
sheet in 350°F oven for 15 min.

Makes 36

ALMOND-SAUSAGE CHEESE TARTS

Pastry:
1 cup butter or margarine, softened
1 package (8 ounces) cream
   cheese, softened
1 tablespoon chopped chives
1 teaspoon salt
3 cups sifted all-purpose flour

In medium-size bowl cream butter,
cream cheese, chives and salt.
Work in flour with a fork or pastry
blender. Divide dough in half;
shape into balls, wrap in waxed
paper and refrigerate one hour.
Roll each ball on sheet of
aluminum foil into 12 × 15-inch
rectangle, about ⅛-inch thick. Cut
pastry and foil together with
scissors into 1½ × 3-inch
rectangles. Moisten ends with
water; pinch together; spread out
slightly into canoe-shape. Prick
pastry well with fork to keep its
shape. Place on cookie sheet. Bake
in 400 degree F. oven 12 to 15
minutes or until golden. Remove
foil. Prepare Almond-Sausage
Filling*. Baked pastries may be

wrapped and frozen, unfilled, up to 2 weeks. *Makes about 7 dozen*

Food Processor Directions: Place metal blade in processor bowl; add chilled butter (do not soften) and cream cheese (each cut into pieces); process until blended. Remove cover and add chives, salt and flour; mix until well blended. Remove dough from bowl, wrap in waxed paper, chill one hour. Proceed as directed above. (Depending on your processor, it may be easiest to do in two batches.)

*Almond-Sausage Filling:
1½ **pounds medium-spiced pork**
    sausage
⅓ **cup BLUE DIAMOND® Whole**
    Blanched Almonds, finely
    chopped
½ **cup sliced green onion**
Salt, pepper and garlic powder
2 **tablespoons hot mustard**
1 **egg**

In large skillet, brown meat, almonds and onion; season with salt, pepper and garlic powder to taste; remove from heat. Beat together mustard and egg and stir into meat mixture. Spoon into baked pastries. Bake in 375 degree F. oven for 10 minutes. Serve warm or at room temperature.

HOT CHICKEN AND CHEESE CANAPÉS

1 can (5 ounces) SWANSON
Chunk Chicken
¼ cup shredded Cheddar cheese
¼ cup chopped celery
3 tablespoons mayonnaise
1 tablespoon chopped parsley
⅛ teaspoon hot pepper sauce

Combine ingredients; spread on crackers or toast squares. Broil 4″ from heat until cheese melts.

Makes about 1 cup

CHEESE PUFFS LINDSAY®

2 egg whites
⅛ teaspoon salt
1 (7½ oz.) can LINDSAY®
Chopped Ripe Olives
¼ cup mayonnaise
2 tablespoons crisp bacon bits

2 tablespoons finely chopped
   onion
2 to 3 drops liquid red pepper
   seasoning
36 small toast rounds
Grated Parmesan cheese

Beat egg whites with salt until
stiff. Fold in chopped ripe olives,
mayonnaise, bacon bits, onion and
pepper seasoning. Pile onto toast
rounds and sprinkle with cheese.
Bake in hot oven (400 degrees F.)
about 10 to 12 minutes until puffed
and lightly browned. Serve hot.

Makes about 3 dozen

JAYS CHEESE PUFFS

1½ cups grated Cheddar cheese
2 egg yolks
1 teaspoon Worcestershire sauce
2 egg whites
½ cup finely crushed JAYS
   Potato Chips
Whole JAYS Potato Chips

Add beaten egg yolks and
Worcestershire sauce to cheese.
Combine with beaten egg whites
and fold in crushed potato chips.
Place small amount of mixture on
whole potato chips and bake in 400
degree oven until puffed and brown
(5 to 6 minutes). Serve at once.

Campbell Soup Company

CHEDDAR CHICKEN PUFFS WITH TARRAGON SOUR CREAM

1 can (11 ounces) CAMPBELL'S
  Condensed Cheddar Cheese
  Soup
1 can (5 ounces) SWANSON Chunk
  Style Mixin' Chicken
1 egg, slightly beaten
½ cup Italian flavored fine dry
  bread crumbs
2 tablespoons finely chopped
  green pepper
2 tablespoons finely chopped
  green onions
¼ teaspoon hot pepper sauce
Salad oil
¼ cup sour cream
Generous dash crushed tarragon
  leaves

In bowl, mix *thoroughly* ¼ cup
soup, chicken, egg, bread crumbs,
green pepper, green onions and
hot pepper sauce. Shape into 40
small chicken meatballs (½ inch).
Roll in additional bread crumbs.
Half-fill deep fat fryer or large
saucepan with oil; preheat to
350°F. Fry meatballs, a few at a
time, in hot oil until browned.

Drain; keep warm. Meanwhile, in saucepan, combine remaining soup, sour cream and tarragon. Heat; stir occasionally. Serve with meatballs. *Makes 40 appetizers*

BROCCOLI PUFFS

10-oz. pkg. GREEN GIANT® Cut Broccoli Frozen in Cheese Sauce
1½ cups yellow cornmeal
½ cup flour
2 tablespoons sugar
1½ teaspoons garlic salt
1¼ teaspoons baking powder
1 teaspoon salt
¾ cup milk
1 egg
Oil for deep frying

Cook broccoli according to package directions. Empty contents into small bowl and cut broccoli, using 2 knives, into ½-inch pieces. Lightly spoon flour into measuring cup; level off. In medium bowl, combine cornmeal, flour, sugar, garlic salt, baking powder and salt. Stir in broccoli with cheese sauce, milk and egg; batter should be fairly thick. Allow batter to set 5 to 10 minutes. In deep fat fryer or heavy saucepan drop batter by teaspoonfuls into 1

continued

continued

to 1½-inches hot fat (375°F.). Fry
until golden brown, turning once.
Drain on paper towel.

48 appetizers

FINNTASTIC CHEESE BLISTERS

1 cup flour
¼ teaspoon salt
Generous dash cayenne pepper
½ cup butter or margarine
**1 cup grated FINLANDIA Swiss
   Cheese**
3 tablespoons ice water

In large mixing bowl, combine
flour, salt and pepper. Using pastry
blender or 2 knives, cut butter and
cheese into flour until mixture
resembles coarse meal. Gradually
add cold water, mixing well with
fork after each addition. On lightly
floured board, roll pastry very thin.
Using sharp knife, cut into 3 by
½-inch strips. Place on ungreased
baking sheets. Bake at 425°F.
about 10 minutes, until golden
brown.   *Makes about 5 dozen*

CHEESE STICKS

1 pkg. refrigerator crescent rolls
1 egg, beaten

**1½ cups shredded FINLANDIA
  Swiss Cheese**

Place perforated strips of
refrigerator dough side by side and
seal edges to form a large
rectangle. Brush egg over surface
of dough and sprinkle generously
with cheese. Cut into sticks about
4 × 1 in. Place sticks on baking
sheet and bake at 400 deg. 15 min.
or until cheese is puffy and golden.

Note: Puff pastry or pie pastry
       dough may be substituted
       for the rolls.

CHEESE STRAWS

**2 cups (8 ozs.) shredded CRACKER
  BARREL Brand Sharp Natural
  Cheddar Cheese**
⅓ cup PARKAY Margarine
1 teaspoon Worcestershire sauce
¼ teaspoon salt
1 cup flour

Heat oven to 375°. Thoroughly
blend cheese and margarine; stir in
Worcestershire sauce and salt.
Add flour; mix well. Roll dough
between two sheets of waxed
paper to ⅛-inch thickness; cut into
3 × 1-inch strips. Place on lightly
greased cookie sheets. Bake at
375°, 12 minutes.   *3 dozen*

CRUNCHY TOAST STICKS

4 slices white bread, toasted
⅓ cup crumbled CHEEZ-IT®
   Crackers
¼ cup grated Romano cheese
½ teaspoon onion salt
⅓ cup butter, softened
   at room temperature

Remove crust from toast slices.
Cut each slice into 4 long sticks.
Combine cracker crumbs with
cheese. Mix onion salt with butter.
Roll each toast stick first in the
butter and then in the cracker-
cheese mixture. Bake on
ungreased cookie sheet in 400°F.
oven for 5 minutes or until crisp.
Serve immediately.   *Yield: 16 sticks*

CHIPPY CHEESE
STRAWS

1 package pie crust mix
⅔ cup grated sharp Cheddar
   cheese
1 cup finely crushed JAYS Potato
   Chips
1 egg white
Salt and cayenne

Prepare pie crust according to package directions, roll very thin and in square shape if possible. Combine cheese with potato chips and sprinkle half of dough with half of mixture. Fold over. Sprinkle remaining mixture on one-half of folded dough. Fold again. Roll out to one-quarter inch thickness. Brush with egg white and sprinkle with salt and cayenne. Cut in strips ½-inch by 6 inches. Bake at 450 degrees until crisp and golden brown.

CHEESY PEANUT STRIPS

1 (8-ounce) package DROMEDARY Corn Muffin Mix
1 egg
⅓ cup milk
½ cup chopped salted peanuts
6 ounces Cheddar cheese, shredded (about 1½ cups)
1 (2-ounce) jar DROMEDARY Diced Pimientos, drained

Prepare corn muffin mix according to package directions, using egg and milk. Reserve 2 tablespoons peanuts; stir remainder into batter. Spread into a greased 13 × 9 × 2-inch baking pan. Sprinkle with combined cheese and pimientos and then reserved

continued

continued

peanuts. Bake in preheated moderate oven (375°F.) about 20 minutes or until done. Cut into strips and serve warm.

Makes 24 (about 3 × 1¼-inch) strips

SURPRISE SAUSAGE BARBECUE

8 ounce package SWIFT PREMIUM® BROWN 'N SERVE® Sausage Links, cut into thirds
½ cup grape jelly
½ teaspoon cornstarch
½ cup catsup

Brown sausage according to package directions. Drain. In a small saucepan mix together a small amount of grape jelly with the cornstarch. Blend well. Add remaining jelly and catsup. Cook over medium heat, stirring constantly, until mixture thickens slightly and begins to boil. Continue to cook and stir 1 minute. Pour mixture into a chafing dish or into a heatproof dish on a hot tray. Add sausages and stir to coat. Serve with wooden picks.

Yield: 30 appetizers

GRUYERE DELIGHTS

2 packages (6 ounces each)
   VALIO Gruyere wedges
Flour
1 egg, slightly beaten
Fine dry bread crumbs
⅓ cup butter or margarine
Dark pumpernickel bread

Remove foil from wedges of
cheese. Dredge in flour, then egg,
then bread crumbs. Heat butter
until very hot in skillet. Sauté
cheese wedges, turning only once.
(Cheese must be crisp on the
outside and melted on inside.)
Total cooking time is not more
than 5 minutes. Serve with
pumpernickel bread.

Makes 6 to 8 servings

STRUDEL A LA SUOMI

1 package (10 ounces) frozen puff
   pastry
2 tablespoons butter or margarine,
   softened
1½ cups shredded FINLANDIA
   Swiss Cheese
1½ cups dairy sour cream
1 can (4½ ounces) devilled ham
1 egg, well beaten

continued

continued

Defrost pastry in refrigerator overnight. Place 3 shells side by side on floured board. Place 2 shells side by side on top of center patty shell. Cut remaining shell in half and place one half on either side of the 2 rounds on top. Roll out to 8 × 14 inch rectangle. Brush with butter. Combine cheese, sour cream and ham. Add ½ beaten egg. Pile mixture along 14 inch side. Roll up, jelly roll fashion. Pinch ends to seal. Place on greased cookie sheet. Brush with remaining egg. Bake at 400°F. for 35 minutes. Cool.

Makes 28 ½-inch slices

WILD TURKEY LIQUEUR ®

WILD WIENERS

In large skillet combine 1 bottle (14 oz.) catsup and 1 cup WILD TURKEY Liqueur. Simmer uncovered 15 minutes. Add 2 lbs. miniature cocktail frankfurters or 4 cans (9 oz.) Vienna sausages. Continue simmering 15 minutes. Serve in chafing dish with picks. Makes an easy yet delicious appetizer.

HIBACHI APPETIZER KABOBS

1 pkg. (5 oz.) OSCAR MAYER
  Brand Little Wieners
1 pkg. (5½ oz.) OSCAR MAYER
  Brand Little Smokies Sausage
1 can (8 oz.) pineapple chunks,
  reserve liquid
1 lemon, sliced
2 oranges, cut into wedges
6-inch metal skewers

Thread skewers alternating Little
Wieners, Little Smokies and fruits.
Grill on hibachi. Brush with Honey
Sauce;* turn occasionally until
heated through.   *Makes 8*

*HONEY SAUCE

⅓ cup pineapple liquid (reserved
  from canned pineapple chunks)
¼ cup honey
1 Tbsp. lemon juice
2 tsp. cornstarch
½ tsp. celery seed
¼ tsp. paprika

Combine all ingredients in
saucepan; heat to boiling, stirring
constantly. Cook until thickened.
Use to brush on kabobs.
          Makes ½ cup

LITTLE WIENERS IN ORANGE SAUCE

1 cup sugar
3 tablespoons cornstarch
8 whole cloves
¼ teaspoon cinnamon
1½ cups orange juice
¼ cup vinegar
2 packages (5 oz. each) OSCAR MAYER Brand Little Smokies Sausage
2 packages (5½ oz. each) OSCAR MAYER Brand Little Wieners

Mix sugar, cornstarch, cloves and cinnamon in saucepan or chafing dish. Add orange juice and vinegar. Cook over medium heat, stirring constantly, until thick. Add little links and cook slowly 5 minutes longer, or until heated through. Keep warm over low heat in chafing dish. Use picks for serving.
Makes 64 appetizers

LITTLE WIENERS WELLINGTON

1 pkg. (4 oz.) OSCAR MAYER Braunschweiger
1 9-inch frozen pie shell
1 pkg. (5½ oz.) OSCAR MAYER Brand Little Wieners

Allow braunschweiger to soften at room temperature, about 30 min. Thaw pie shell about 10 min.; remove from pan, flatten and repair any cracks. Spread with braunschweiger. Cut into five strips; cut the two end strips in half; cut three center strips into fourths. Roll each piece of dough around little wiener, pinching seam to seal. Place seam side down on baking sheet. Bake in 375°F oven for 20 min. until lightly browned.

Makes 16

HOT BEEF 'N FRANK TIDBITS*

1 pound ground lean beef
1 egg, lightly beaten
¼ cup soft bread crumbs
3 tablespoons LEA & PERRINS Worcestershire Sauce, divided
2 tablespoons catsup, divided
¼ teaspoon salt
1/16 teaspoon TABASCO® Sauce
2 tablespoons oil
½ cup red currant jelly
1 jar (6 oz.) cocktail frankfurters, drained

In a mixing bowl combine beef, egg, bread crumbs, 1 tablespoon each of the LEA & PERRINS and catsup, salt and TABASCO®. Mix

continued

continued

well, but do not overmix. Shape
into 1-inch balls. In a large skillet
heat oil. Add meatballs and brown
well on all sides. Remove and drain
on paper towels. Discard fat from
skillet. In same skillet combine
jelly, remaining 2 tablespoons LEA
& PERRINS and 1 tablespoon
catsup. Heat and stir until jelly
melts. Add meatballs and
frankfurters. Cover and cook 10
minutes, stirring occasionally, until
mixture bubbles.

*Yield: about 35 meatballs and 12
frankfurters*

*May be prepared in advance of
serving.

PORK SAUSAGE
WONTONS

**1 pkg. (1 lb.) OSCAR MAYER
Ground Pork Sausage
1 can (8 oz.) water chestnuts,
drained, finely chopped
2 green onions, finely chopped
30 wonton skins, 3½-inch square
Peanut or vegetable oil for frying**

In skillet cook sausage over
medium heat about 12 min.,
stirring and separating sausage as
it cooks; drain on absorbent paper.
Combine sausage, water chestnuts

and onion. Place 1 Tbsp. sausage mixture on center of wonton skin. Moisten corners of wonton skin with water and fold up over sausage mixture like an envelope. Pinch to seal.* Heat at least 1-inch oil in heavy skillet, wok or deep fat fryer to 375°F. Fry wontons until golden brown, turning once. Drain on absorbent paper. Serve with sweet and sour sauce and Chinese hot mustard.   *Makes 30*

*Wontons and skins should be covered with moist towel when they are not being handled; they have a tendency to dry out and become brittle.

HAM CORDON BLEU

1 pkg. (6 oz.) OSCAR MAYER
  Smoked Cooked Ham (square)
2 Tbsp. bottled horseradish sauce
1 pkg. (6 oz.) OSCAR MAYER
  Sliced Turkey Breast Meat
8 slices natural Swiss cheese,
  each 4-inches square
¼ cup butter, melted
½ cup crushed herb seasoned
  stuffing mix

Spread each slice of ham with horseradish sauce; top with turkey slice and cheese. Roll and secure

continued

continued

with picks. Brush with melted
butter and roll in seasoned
crumbs. Place on baking sheet and
heat in 350°F oven for 12 min. until
cheese just begins to melt.
Remove picks; cut into ½-inch
slices. Serve warm.

Microwave in 12 × 7-inch glass
baking dish covered with plastic
wrap (turning back corner to vent)
for 3½-4 minutes.   *Makes 64*

GINGER PORK BALLS IN SHERRY-ORANGE SAUCE

1 large slice white bread, crumbled
   (about 1 cup crumbs)
¼ cup THE CHRISTIAN
   BROTHERS® Golden Sherry
1½ pounds lean ground pork
½ cup minced water chestnuts
2 tablespoons soy sauce
1 egg yolk
2 teaspoons ground ginger
1 large clove garlic, crushed
Sherry-Orange Sauce (recipe
   follows)

In large bowl combine bread and
sherry; set aside 10 minutes. Add
remaining ingredients except
Sherry-Orange Sauce. Mix to blend
thoroughly. Cover and chill at least

30 minutes. Form into 1-inch balls. Place slightly apart on baking sheet. Bake in 400 degree oven about 20 minutes until cooked through and lightly browned. Meanwhile prepare Sherry-Orange Sauce. Add drained pork balls to sauce. Cook over medium heat until hot through, stirring gently. Remove from heat; gently stir in orange segments (reserved in Sherry-Orange Sauce recipe). Serve hot with cocktail picks for spearing.   *Makes about 5 dozen*

SHERRY-ORANGE SAUCE

2 cans (11 ounces *each*) mandarin orange segments
¾ cup chicken broth or bouillon
⅓ cup THE CHRISTIAN BROTHERS® Golden Sherry
2 tablespoons *each* cornstarch and soy sauce

Drain liquid from orange segments into 2-cup measure; reserve segments. Add broth to orange liquid to make 2 cups. Pour into 2-quart saucepan. Mix sherry, cornstarch and soy sauce; add to saucepan. Cook and stir over medium heat until smooth and thickened. Simmer 1 minute.

First Prize winner THE CHRISTIAN BROTHERS® contest

SESAME PORK TIDBITS WITH SWEET & SOUR SAUCE

1 ½ pounds boneless pork loin
½ cup cornstarch
¼ cup KIKKOMAN Teriyaki Sauce
3 tablespoons sesame seed,
  lightly toasted
3 cups vegetable oil

Sweet & Sour Sauce:
¼ cup sugar
¼ cup vinegar
¼ cup catsup
¼ cup water
1 tablespoon KIKKOMAN Teriyaki
  Sauce
1 ½ teaspoons cornstarch

Trim excess fat from pork; cut into
1-inch cubes and set aside.
Thoroughly combine cornstarch,
teriyaki sauce and sesame seed in
medium-size bowl (mixture will be
very stiff). Stir in pork cubes and
let stand 30 minutes. Meanwhile,
combine all ingredients for Sweet
& Sour Sauce in saucepan. Cook
over high heat, stirring constantly,

until thickened; set aside and keep warm. Heat oil in medium-size saucepan over medium-high heat to 300°F. Add ⅓ of the pork pieces and cook, stirring occasionally, until golden brown (approximately 2 minutes). Remove and drain thoroughly on paper towels. Repeat with remaining pork. Serve immediately with warm Sweet & Sour Sauce.

Makes approximately 3 dozen appetizers

SAUSAGE WITH HOT MUSTARD SAUCE

**8 ounce package SWIFT PREMIUM®
BROWN 'N SERVE® Sausage
Links**

Cut sausage links into halves. Brown according to package directions. Keep hot on hot tray or in chafing dish. Spear sausage pieces with smooth wooden picks. Serve with Hot Mustard Sauce* for a dip.   *Yield: 20 appetizers*

*HOT MUSTARD SAUCE

**2 tablespoons butter or margarine
1 tablespoon flour
½ teaspoon salt**

continued

continued

1 cup water
1 beef bouillon cube
⅓ cup Dijon-style mustard
2 teaspoons horseradish
2 tablespoons sugar

Melt butter in a saucepan. Stir in flour
and salt. Gradually add water. Add
bouillon cube, mustard, horseradish
and sugar. Stir and cook until sauce
thickens. *Yield: 1½ cups*

FRUIT 'N' TURKEY RUMAKI

36 half inch chunks roast
    BUTTERBALL® SWIFT'S
    PREMIUM® Turkey
18 slices SWIFT PREMIUM®
    Bacon, cut in half crosswise
36 chunks pineapple
Sweet Sour Sauce*

Partially cook bacon. Drain. Top
each chunk of turkey with
pineapple, wrap with a half slice of
bacon and place on skewer. Place
on outdoor grill 2 to 3 minutes until
bacon is crisp. Dip into Sweet Sour
Sauce before serving.
                    Yield: 36 appetizers

Broiling directions: Place
appetizers on rack in shallow pan
and broil 4 to 5 minutes.

*SWEET SOUR SAUCE

1 cup brown sugar
2 tablespoons cornstarch
¼ teaspoon salt
¼ teaspoon ground cinnamon
Dash ground cloves
6 ounce can pineapple juice
½ cup white wine vinegar
¼ cup lime juice

Combine sugar, cornstarch, salt
and spices in a small saucepan.
Gradually stir in pineapple juice,
vinegar and lime juice. Cook over
medium-low heat, stirring
constantly until thick and clear.

Yield: 1¾ cups

TURKEY RUMAKI
SPANISH STYLE

36 half inch chunks roast
   BUTTERBALL® SWIFT'S
   PREMIUM® Turkey
18 slices SWIFT SIZZLEAN®
36 small pimiento stuffed olives

Follow directions on package for
cooking SIZZLEAN®, frying only 2
minutes on each side. Drain. Cut
each slice in halves crosswise.
Place an olive on each turkey
chunk, wrap with a half slice of
SIZZLEAN®. Place on skewer.

continued

Place on outdoor grill 2 to 3 minutes or until SIZZLEAN® is cooked. *Yield: 36 appetizers*

Broiling directions: Place appetizers on rack in shallow pan and broil 4 to 5 minutes. Serve hot.

SHRIMP TOAST

**1 can (4½ ounces) LOUISIANA
  BRAND Shrimp
2 eggs
1 tablespoon cornstarch
1 teaspoon sugar
2 teaspoons dry sherry (optional)
⅓ cup finely chopped celery
6 slices bread, slightly stale
Salad oil**

Drain and chop shrimp. Whisk together eggs, cornstarch, sugar, wine. Add celery and shrimp. Spread mixture on bread, pressing and smoothing with the back of a spoon until it clings. Fill deep-fry pan with salad oil to a depth of 2 inches or enough to float slices and brown without turning. Heat oil to 375 degrees or until it will brown a bread cube almost instantly. Fry slices *one at a time* about 15 seconds, shrimp side *down*. Drain on absorbent paper. Cut in triangles.

Makes 12 or 24 hot appetizers

PEPPERIDGE FARM®
PATTY SHELL
HORS D'OEUVRES

Roll each thawed PEPPERIDGE FARM® Patty Shell to ⅛ inch thickness. Cut with a sharp knife into diamonds, squares, triangles and long narrow strips. Bake at 400°F. for 10 to 15 minutes or until puffed and brown. Cool and then top with desired filling. Use deviled ham topped with red caviar, chicken spread topped with olive slices, liver spread topped with crumbled crisp bacon, tartar sauce spread topped with tiny shrimp, melted butter sprinkled with celery salt, garlic salt and onion salt. Or spoon on a little canned cherry pie filling, topped with whipped cream and slices of strawberries.

Cut 2 inch squares of the ⅛ inch thick puff pastry and top with a whole mushroom (canned), or a whole olive, or a cube of Cheddar, or cooked shrimp, or a piece of chicken liver or cube of ham. Brush edge with egg and fold over into a triangle. Bake at 400°F. for 15 to 20 minutes or until puffed and brown. Serve hot.

SARDINE SPIRALS

2 cans KING OSCAR Sardines, drained
4 tsp. lemon juice
¾ tsp. prepared horseradish
Bread, sliced ¼″ thick
Melted butter
Grated Parmesan cheese

Mash sardines with lemon juice and horseradish. Trim crusts from bread. Spread mixture on bread slices. Roll bread up, cut in half crosswise, fasten with picks. Brush with melted butter, sprinkle with Parmesan. Place on shallow pan; toast quickly in hot oven (475°).

HOT BACON SPREAD

1 package (8 oz.) OSCAR MAYER Bacon
2 packages (3 oz. each) cream cheese
2 tablespoons milk
2 tablespoons finely chopped onion
½ teaspoon horseradish

Preheat oven to 375°. Cook bacon until crisp; drain and crumble. Blend cream cheese with milk. Stir in onion, horseradish and crumbled bacon*. Spread in individual

casserole or small ovenproof
platter. Bake 15 minutes. Serve
with crackers or fresh vegetable
relishes.   *Makes 1 cup*

*A few tablespoons of bacon may
 be reserved to sprinkle on top of
 mixture before baking.

DEVILED SPREAD

2 cans KING OSCAR Sardines,
   drained
8 slices whole wheat bread
2 tsp. prepared mustard with
   horseradish
2 Tbsp. finely minced Bermuda or
   sweet onion
1 Tbsp. mayonnaise
1 tsp. Worcestershire sauce
1 tsp. lemon juice
½ tsp. grated lemon peel
¾ cup grated Cheddar cheese

Mash sardines and mix with all
remaining ingredients except
cheese and bread. Remove crusts
from bread and toast both sides.
Spread toast with sardine mixture,
then cut each slice into 3 pieces.
Place closely together on baking
sheet; sprinkle grated cheese on
each piece. Put into broiler until
cheese melts. Serve hot.
                        Makes 24

PICKLE POCKETS

2 cups finely grated American
  cheese
½ cup softened butter or
  margarine
1 cup all-purpose flour
Dash cayenne
HEINZ Dill or Sweet Pickles

Mix cheese and butter well. Using
pastry blender, cut in flour and
cayenne. Divide into 2 balls; chill.
Cut 36 strips (2″ × ½″) from
Pickles. Roll each ball to ⅛″
thickness on floured board; cut in
rectangles (2½″ × 2″). Wrap each
Pickle strip in dough; seal ends
well. Place on ungreased baking
sheets. Bake in 425°F. oven, 12-15
minutes.   *Makes 3 dozen*

THE KING IN A BLANKET

1 can KING OSCAR Sardines
1 can refrigerated crescent rolls
¼ tsp. dry mustard

¼ tsp. onion powder
2 Tbsp. lemon juice

Drain sardines and reserve oil in
small dish. Open crescent rolls,
unroll crescents and cut each one
in half. Mix mustard, onion powder,
lemon juice into sardine oil. Spread
mixture on each crescent, not
quite to edge. Lay 2 whole sardines
on each crescent half, roll up,
pinch edges together lightly. Place
on cookie sheet, bake at 400°
about 10 to 12 minutes, until
brown. If desired, spear a green
pimiento-stuffed olive on a
toothpick and place on top of each
sardine roll. Serve piping hot.

NALLEY®'S NACHOS

NALLEY®'S Tortilla Chips
2 to 4 tablespoons diced
    NALLEY®'S Jalapeno Peppers
    or NALLEY®'S Hot Chili
    Peppers
1 4-ounce can sliced or chopped
    olives
½ pound shredded or sliced
    Muenster or Jack cheese
Guacamole, sour cream and
    picante sauce or salsa

Spread single layer of tortilla chips
on baking sheet. Sprinkle evenly

continued

continued

with peppers, olives and cheese.
Broil about 4-inches from heat until
cheese is melted, about 1 ½ to 2
minutes. Serve hot with
guacamole, sour cream and
picante sauce or salsa.

JIMMY DEAN® NACHOS

1 lb. JIMMY DEAN® Seasoned Taco
  Filling
2 Tbsp. tomato paste
1 bag tortilla chips
1 cup cheddar cheese
Jalapeños to taste

Sauté JIMMY DEAN® Seasoned
Taco Filling until brown and
crumbly. Add 2 Tbsp. tomato
paste. Spread on tortilla chips. Top
with grated cheese. Broil till
melted. Garnish with jalapeño.
Optional: Top with 1 tsp.
guacamole.

OLD EL PASO® NACHOS

1 box (7½ oz.) OLD EL PASO®
  NACHIPS Tortilla Chips
1 can (16 oz.) OLD EL PASO®
  Refried Beans or OLD EL
  PASO® Refried Beans with
  Green Chilies or OLD EL PASO®
  Refried Beans with Sausage

1 can (4 oz.) **OLD EL PASO**® Chopped Green Chilies or 1 jar (11½ oz.) **OLD EL PASO**® Jalapeno Strips
2½ cups (10 oz.) shredded Cheddar or Monterey Jack cheese

Spread tortilla chips on a large baking sheet. Top each with beans and a few green chilies or a slice of jalapeno pepper. Sprinkle each with a tablespoon of cheese. Place under broiler until cheese melts, about 2 to 3 minutes. Serve immediately.

Microwave instructions: Microcook on full power until cheese is melted, about 2-3 minutes. Time will vary with the number of nachos prepared.

Hunt's®

CHILIES CON QUESO

½ lb. process American cheese, cut into ½-inch cubes
1 (6 oz.) can HUNT'S Tomato Paste
1 cup water
1 (4-oz.) can diced green chilies
½ cup minced onion
¼ cup diced green pepper
2 tsp. lemon juice

continued

continued

¼ tsp. TABASCO®
Tortilla or corn chips

In a saucepan, melt cheese over
low heat. Meanwhile, combine
remaining ingredients *except*
tortilla chips in a small bowl; stir
into melted cheese. Serve in
fondue pot or chafing dish with
tortilla chips.   *Makes 1 quart*

CITRUS SCOOP-OUTS
(Low Sodium)

2 medium grapefruit
2 medium oranges
⅓ cup honey
2 tablespoons FLEISCHMANN'S®
  Unsalted Margarine, melted
Pinch curry powder
½ cup chopped PLANTERS® Dry
  Roasted Unsalted Mixed Nuts

Cut grapefruit in half; remove
sections and reserve. Remove and
discard membrane from grapefruit
shells; set shells aside. Peel and
section oranges.

In a medium bowl mix honey,
FLEISCHMANN'S® Unsalted
Margarine and curry powder; fold
in grapefruit, orange sections and
PLANTERS® Dry Roasted Unsalted
Mixed Nuts. Spoon fruit mixture

into grapefruit shells and place in a shallow baking dish.

Bake at 450°F. for 15 minutes, or until hot. Serve warm, garnished with fresh mint leaves if desired.

4 servings

Per serving: 310 calories, 5 mg. sodium

BROILED RUBY REDS

2 Texas Ruby Red Grapefruit, halved
¼ cup IMPERIAL Brown Sugar
¼ teaspoon cinnamon
¼ cup shredded coconut
Maraschino cherries

Cut around each section with grapefruit knife. Combine IMPERIAL Brown Sugar and cinnamon and spread over grapefruit. Broil until juice is bubbling. Sprinkle with shredded coconut and broil until coconut is toasted. Add cherries to centers of grapefruit.　　*Makes 4 servings*

NOR'EAST NIBBLES

16 frozen BOOTH Fish Sticks
½ cup grated Parmesan cheese
2 tablespoons butter or margarine
Sea Sauce*

Preheat oven to 450°. Cut frozen
fish sticks into thirds. Roll each
piece in cheese. Melt butter in a
baking pan, 15″ × 10″ × 1″. Place
fish in pan. Bake 8 to 10 minutes.
Turn carefully. Bake 8 to 10
minutes longer or until crisp and
brown. Drain on absorbent paper.
Serve with hot Sea Sauce.
Makes 48 hors d'oeuvres

*SEA SAUCE

1 can (8 ounces) tomato sauce
¼ cup chili sauce
¼ teaspoon garlic powder
¼ teaspoon oregano
¼ teaspoon liquid hot pepper
** sauce**
¼ teaspoon thyme
⅛ teaspoon sugar
Dash basil

Combine all ingredients. Simmer
10 to 12 minutes, stirring
occasionally.
Makes 1 cup sauce

Quickie Appetizers

SAVORY DEVILED CHEESE SPREAD

Juicy Bartlett wedges "pear" with this savory deviled cheese spread for a refreshing appetizer. Blend together 1 package (3 oz.) softened cream cheese, 2 tablespoons crumbled blue cheese and 1 can (2¼ oz.) deviled ham. Chill several hours to blend flavors.

Makes about ½ cup spread

Favorite recipe from Pacific Bartlett Growers, Inc.

PIGGY WRAPS

Cut HILLSHIRE FARM® Sausage into desired shapes. Wrap in refrigerated crescent dough. Bake at 400° for 5 minutes or until golden brown. May be frozen. To reheat in microwave, microwave uncovered, HIGH 1½ minutes or MEDIUM HIGH 2 minutes. When reheated in microwave, pastry will not be crisp.

CHEESE STUFFED CELERY

Pipe 1 (4¾-ounce) can SNACK MATE Pasteurized Process Cheese Spread Cheddar onto 4 stalks celery. Cut into 1½-inch pieces. Stand a CORN DIGGERS Snack in end of each. Sprinkle with paprika, if desired.

Makes 24 (about 1½-inch) pieces

DATE CARROT CURLS

Using vegetable parer, cut about 36 thin lengthwise strips from raw carrots (about 6). Roll each strip into a curl and fasten with a wooden pick. Chill in ice water several hours. Drain; remove picks and stuff each with a date using 1 (8-ounce) package DROMEDARY Pitted Dates; re-insert picks through dates. To serve: Remove picks; sprinkle lightly with salt.

Makes about 3 dozen

ITALIAN NACHOS

Place thinly sliced HILLSHIRE FARM® Italian Smoked Sausage on tortilla chips. Top with Monterey Jack or taco flavored

cheese. Broil until cheese melts or
arrange in circle and microwave
uncovered, HIGH 15 seconds or
MEDIUM HIGH 20 seconds. If
desired, garnish with sour cream.

GRECIAN TOUCH

Marinate chunks from 1 lb.
HILLSHIRE FARM® Sausage in
juice of 1 fresh lemon and 1 tsp.
crushed oregano for at least 30
minutes. Bake, covered at 350° for
30 minutes or microwave, covered,
HIGH 6-8 minutes, stirring once.
Serve with toothpicks.

SWEET & SAUCY

Heat equal parts of currant jelly
and catsup in saucepan, or
microwave, uncovered, HIGH 1-2
minutes until mixture can be
blended smooth. Add bite size
pieces of HILLSHIRE FARM®
Sausage and heat until sausage is
hot. Serve with toothpicks.

SMOKEY TIDBITS

Tuck slivers of smoked salmon
inside big shiny black LINDSAY®
Pitted Ripe Olives, add a tassle of
parsley and serve on picks.

FIRESIDE SNACK

Top PREMIUM Saltine Crackers
with American cheese and
miniature frankfurters. Toast in
toaster-oven until cheese is
melted.

Lindsay®

LINDSAY® RIPE OLIVE "FILLERS"

A quick and easy appetizer to
spread on crackers or melba toast
is prepared by combining 1 (3 oz.)
package of cream cheese, ¼ cup
LINDSAY® Chopped Ripe Olives, 1
(2¼ oz.) can deviled ham and ½ to
1 teaspoon horseradish.

CANAPÉ A LA CAVALIER

Upon white bread, cut in fancy
shapes, spread a mixture of equal
parts of AMBER BRAND Deviled
SMITHFIELD Ham and
PHILADELPHIA BRAND Cream
Cheese. Decorate with slices of
stuffed green olives.

PIMIENTO DEVILED EGGS

Drain 1 (2-ounce) jar DROMEDARY Sliced Pimientos. Finely chop enough to make 1 tablespoon chopped. Cut 6 hard-cooked eggs in half lengthwise. Remove yolks and mash. Combine with 2 tablespoons mayonnaise, the chopped pimiento, 2 teaspoons cider vinegar and ⅛ teaspoon salt. Stuff egg whites and garnish with remaining sliced pimientos.

Makes 12

SAUSAGE BALLS

In large bowl combine 1 pkg. (1 lb.) OSCAR MAYER Ground Pork Sausage, 3 cups buttermilk baking mix and 1 lb. shredded Cheddar cheese. Knead ingredients together to form soft dough. Shape into 1-inch balls. Place on ungreased baking sheet. Bake 20 min. in 350°F oven until golden brown. Serve hot. Reheat cooked frozen sausage balls 10 min. in 350°F oven.

Makes 72

SAUCY SUGGESTIONS

Add OSCAR MAYER Brand Little Wieners or Little Smokies Sausage to one of the sauces below. Prepare sauce; add little links and heat about 5 min. longer, stirring occasionally. Serve in chafing dish with picks.

Four pkg. makes 64 appetizers

Little Rubies: Heat together 1 can (21 oz.) cherry pie filling and ¼ cup rosé wine.

Orange Nutmeg: Combine ½ cup sugar with 2 Tbsp. cornstarch and ½ tsp. nutmeg. Stir in 1¼ cups orange juice. Cook over medium heat, stirring constantly until mixture boils and is thickened. Stir in 1 can (11 oz.) mandarin orange segments, drained.

Barbecue: Heat 1 bottle (18 oz.) barbecue sauce.

Currant: Heat 2 jars (10 oz. each) currant jelly.

NACHOS

Arrange tortilla chips on baking sheet. Top each with 1 tsp. OSCAR MAYER Cheese and Bacon Spread and a slice of olive, mild banana pepper or jalapeña pepper. Bake in 400°F oven 5 min.

Microwave 12 chips for 30 seconds.

BRAUNSCHWEIGER PARTY LOG

Remove plastic film from 1 pkg. (8 oz.) OSCAR MAYER Braunschweiger, taking care to retain meat in its log shape. Frost log with 1 pkg. (3 oz.) whipped cream cheese and roll in 1 can (3 oz.) OSCAR MAYER Real Bacon Bits. Chill. Serve with crackers.

WRAP-UPS

Cut OSCAR MAYER Bologna or other sliced cold meats into thirds and wrap around bite-size pieces of dill pickle, cheese, fruit or fresh vegetables. Fasten with a pick. Chill until ready to serve.

RIBBON CUBES

Spread 1 pkg. (8 oz.) OSCAR MAYER Chopped Ham and 2 slices very thin square pumpernickel bread with 1 pkg. (3 oz.) cream cheese and chives. Stack in following order: 3 slices ham, one slice bread, 2 slices ham, one slice bread, 3 slices ham. Wrap tightly and chill. Cut into cubes. Use picks to serve. *Makes 16*

BELLS

Cut round sliced meats like OSCAR MAYER Cotto Salami or Bologna in half. Form into cones; insert cherry tomato, radish, olive or cocktail onion in each and fasten with pick.

BACON TIDBITS

Cut OSCAR MAYER Bacon slices in half and wrap around olives, mushrooms or water chestnuts. Fasten with picks. Bake in 400°F oven about 15 min., until bacon is crisp.

STUFFED PICKLES

Core center of CLAUSSEN Kosher Pickles and stuff with OSCAR MAYER Braunschweiger. Chill several hours. Slice stuffed pickles and serve with picks.

FAMOUS CHEESE SIZZLERS

¼ cup DURKEE Imitation Bacon Bits
1 ½ cups shredded Swiss cheese
¼ cup DURKEE Famous Sauce
¼ cup DURKEE Stuffed Olives, chopped
1 tablespoon DURKEE Freeze-Dried Chives
24 slices party rye

Combine all ingredients except bread. Spread mixture on bread and cut into halves. Broil 4 inches from heat until cheese melts and is lightly brown. *Makes 48 servings*

PRESTO PARTY FRANKS

Slice ECKRICH® Franks into a
mixture of one cup currant jelly
and ¾ cup prepared mustard. Heat
and serve.

Makes about four cups

CELERY LOGS
VIRGINIENNE

Blend thoroughly 4 cups softened
cream cheese with 1 cup AMBER
BRAND Deviled SMITHFIELD Ham.
Fill hollows of celery stalks with
ham and cheese mixture; top with
thin strips of pimiento. Cut into
3-4″ lengths. Chill before service.

FAMOUS ECKRICH®
SLENDER SLICED
PINWHEELS

Stack three slices of your favorite
ECKRICH® Slender Sliced Meat.
Spread softened cream cheese on

the top slice and roll, jelly-roll
fashion. Chill until cheese is firm.
Then place five toothpicks along
loose edge of each roll and cut
between the picks with a very
sharp knife.

Makes about 15 pinwheels

LUNCHEON MEAT PINWHEELS

**1 package (8 oz.) OSCAR MAYER
Luncheon Meat**
**1 package (3 oz.) cream cheese,
softened**

Spread all meat slices with cream
cheese. Roll first slice; join meat
edges to start second slice and
continue to roll slices, one over
another, to make a log. Wrap and
chill thoroughly. Cut into slices ¼
inch thick and serve on rye bread
or crackers.

Makes 16 appetizers

SAUSAGE AND MUSHROOM APPETIZER

Remove the stems from fresh mushrooms and wash mushroom caps. Cut SWIFT PREMIUM® BROWN 'N SERVE® Sausage Links into thirds. Place mushroom caps in a shallow pan or on a broiler rack, smooth side up. Brush each with melted butter. Broil about 5 inches from the heat source for 3 minutes. Turn and brush with melted butter. Place ⅓ sausage link in center of each mushroom cap. Broil 2 minutes. Insert a pick in each, making sure to secure sausage and mushroom. Serve hot.

PICKLE KABOBS

Alternate cubes of OSCAR MAYER Cooked Ham and Cheddar cheese with pickle pieces on small skewers.

Dips

SOUTH OF THE BORDER DIP

1 cup SEALTEST® Cottage Cheese
¼ cup medium sharp process
    cheese spread
3 tablespoons chili sauce
½ teaspoon garlic salt

Combine all ingredients, blend
well. Refrigerate in container with
cover.   *1⅓ cups*

SPICY SEAFOOD DIP

1 cup (8 oz.) BREYERS® Plain
    Yogurt
¼ cup mayonnaise
1¼ teaspoons curry powder
1 tablespoon finely chopped onion
2 teaspoons lemon juice
½ teaspoon salt
Dash of pepper
1 can (6½ oz.) crab, tuna fish, or
    shrimp; drained, flaked, or
    chopped

Combine all ingredients; mix well.
Chill several hours. Serve with raw
vegetables or crackers.
                    Makes 1½ cups

Lipton.

LIPTON® CALIFORNIA DIP

In small bowl, blend 1 envelope LIPTON® Onion Soup Mix with 2 cups (16 oz.) sour cream; chill.

Makes about 2 cups

VARIATIONS:

California Vegetable Dip. Add 1 cup each finely chopped green pepper and tomato and 2 teaspoons chili powder.

California Blue Cheese Dip. Add ¼ pound crumbled blue cheese and ¼ cup finely chopped walnuts.

California Seafood Dip. Add 1 cup finely chopped cooked shrimp, clams or crab meat, ¼ cup chili sauce and 1 tablespoon horseradish.

"THE LITTLE MERMAID" DIP

¼ cup mayonnaise
½ cup sour cream
1 can (6½ oz.) tuna, drained & cut in tiny pieces
¼ teaspoon curry

¼ **teaspoon tarragon**
¼ **teaspoon salt**
½ **cup Danish cheese, shredded**
  (Havarti, Esrom, or Tybo)

In medium bowl, blend mayonnaise
& sour cream together. Add tuna,
curry, tarragon & salt. Then add
Danish cheese & blend well.
Refrigerate 1 hour.

Makes about 2 cups dip

*Favorite recipe from Denmark Cheese
Association*

DANABLU DIP WITH NUTS

¼ **cup Danish Blue cheese, at**
  room temperature
⅔ **cup sour cream**
⅓ **cup mayonnaise**
½ **teaspoon salt**
½ **teaspoon chives**
¼ **teaspoon Worcestershire sauce**
1 **clove garlic, mashed**
¼ **cup chopped walnuts**

In medium bowl, mash Danish Blue
cheese with fork. Add ⅓ cup sour
cream & blend thoroughly. Then
fold in remaining ingredients &
refrigerate 1 hour.

Makes about 1½ cups dip

*Favorite recipe from Denmark Cheese
Association*

GREEN AND WHITE DIP FOR JAYS POTATO CHIPS

3 ounces cream cheese (room temperature)
Cream, as needed
1 tablespoon horseradish
¼ teaspoon onion juice or grated onion

Cream ingredients until thoroughly mixed and soft. Use a fork or electric mixer. Add cream to make a "dunking" consistency (serve so that chips can be easily "dunked" in the spread). Add onion and horseradish (more or less may be added to suit the taste). Sprinkle the top of spread with chopped chives or parsley flakes as a garnish. Place the bowl of spread in the center of a large attractive platter and surround with JAYS Potato Chips.

MEXICALI DIP

1 lb. VELVEETA Pasteurized Process Cheese Spread, cubed
1 16-oz. can tomatoes, drained, chopped
1 4-oz. can green chilies, drained, chopped

1 tablespoon instant minced onion
Corn or tortilla chips

Combine process cheese spread,
tomatoes, chilies and onion in
saucepan; cook over low heat until
process cheese spread melts.
Serve hot with corn chips.

3 cups

GUACAMOLE

Mash 2 CALAVO® Avocados. Blend
in a chopped tomato, ¼ cup
grated onion, ½ teaspoon
seasoned salt, 1 tablespoon fresh
CALAVO® Lime Juice. Spread
generously on hamburgers. Or
serve as dip with corn chips. (For
convenience, try CALAVO® Frozen
Fresh Guacamole in flavors.)

Makes 2½ cups

DUBONNET DIP

1 can tuna, mashed
3 3 oz. pkgs. cream cheese
¼ cup DUBONNET Blonde
1 Tbsp. mayonnaise

continued

continued

¼ cup sweet pickle relish, well
   drained
2 tsp. parsley, finely chopped
1 tsp. grated onion
½ tsp. salt
¼ tsp. garlic salt

Soften cream cheese in
DUBONNET. Blend in drained and
mashed tuna. Add remaining
ingredients and mix well.
Refrigerate in covered container.

GREEN GODDESS DIP
FOR JAYS POTATO
CHIPS

1 clove garlic, grated
2 tablespoons anchovy paste
3 tablespoons finely chopped
   chives
1 tablespoon lemon juice
1 tablespoon tarragon wine vinegar
½ cup heavy sour cream
1 cup mayonnaise
⅓ cup finely chopped parsley
Coarse salt
Coarsely ground black pepper

Combine ingredients in order
given. Pour in serving bowl and
chill. Canned whole anchovies may
be chopped fine and substituted
for the anchovy paste. Coarse salt
may be purchased in pound
containers. Lacking a pepper
grinder use a pestle to mash the
peppercorns in a mortar. Serve
with JAYS Potato Chips.

TANGY COCONUT FRUIT DIP

1½ cups COCO CASA™ Cream of
   Coconut
1 can (6 oz.) frozen concentrated
   lemonade, thawed and undiluted
Assorted bite-size fruit pieces such
   as strawberries, pineapple,
   bananas, apples, pears, melon,
   mandarin orange sections, etc.

In a bowl, mix cream of coconut
and lemonade. Stir until well
blended. Chill. Place bowl on
platter surrounded with pieces of
fruit. Spear fruits on skewers or
fondue forks and dip into cream of
coconut mixture. Substitute frozen
concentrated orange juice, pink
lemonade, pineapple juice or lime-
ade for a variety of tastes and
colors.   *Makes about 2½ cups*

CURRIED APPLE AND CHICKEN DIP

1 can (5 ounces) SWANSON Chunk
   Style Mixin' Chicken
½ cup chopped apple
¼ cup chopped almonds
⅓ cup mayonnaise
2 tablespoons chopped raisins
1 tablespoon orange juice
½ teaspoon curry powder

Combine ingredients; chill. Serve
on crackers or as a dip with
assorted vegetables.

Makes about 1 cup

SUNNY PEANUT BUTTER DIP

½ cup SKIPPY® Creamy or Super
   Chunk Peanut Butter
½ cup finely shredded carrot
¼ cup orange juice

In small bowl stir together peanut
butter, carrot and orange juice
until well mixed. Serve as dip for
fresh fruits and vegetables.

Makes about 1 cup

CREAMY CLAM CHEESE DIP

1 cup SEALTEST® Cottage Cheese
2 tablespoons minced, drained
  canned clams
1 teaspoon finely snipped chives
Dash liquid hot-pepper sauce

Blend all ingredients well.
Refrigerate in container with cover.

1 cup

CALIFORNIA SPREAD

1 can KING OSCAR Sardines
1 ripe California avocado
2 Tbsp. grated onion
2 Tbsp. lemon juice
½ cup sour cream
Dash TABASCO®
Salt
Parsley

Mash sardines and avocado. Add
remaining ingredients, except
parsley. Blend thoroughly. Sprinkle
with chopped fresh parsley. Serve
with crackers or toast fingers.

CONFETTI DIP

5 Tbsp. milk
1 pkg. (8 oz.) cream cheese,
    softened
1 Tbsp. chives
2 Tbsp. chopped parsley
2 Tbsp. (1 oz.) ROMANOFF®
    Caviar*

Blend milk with cream cheese until
mixture is easy to dip. Gently stir
in remaining ingredients. Garnish
with additional caviar if desired.
Serve with raw vegetable relishes
(below) or unsalted crackers.

Makes 1¼ cups dip

*ROMANOFF® Red Salmon Caviar
suggested.

RAW VEGETABLE RELISHES

1 bunch celery
1 cucumber
¼ pound very young green beans
4 carrots
½ head cauliflower
1 bunch radishes

Trim celery, wash and separate
out small pieces. Cut large ribs

into three-inch lengths. Peel
cucumber and cut in half
crosswise, then into half-inch
thick strips. Remove ends from
beans. Peel carrots, cut into half-
inch thick strips. Cut cauliflower
into flowerets. Pare radishes.
Place vegetables in ice water at
least one hour. Drain, and serve
with caviar dip.   *Serves 10*

DOUBLE CHEESE BACON DIP

1 cup creamed cottage cheese
1 package (6 ounces) VALIO
  Gruyere Cheese—grated
4 slices bacon, cooked and
  crumbled
2 tablespoons salad dressing
1 teaspoon lemon juice
1 small clove garlic, minced
½ teaspoon red pepper, crushed
2 tablespoons minced green
  pepper
2 tablespoons chopped radishes

Combine cheeses, bacon, salad
dressing, lemon juice, garlic and
red pepper. Stir in green pepper
and radishes. Chill until ready to
serve. Serve as dip for assorted
raw vegetables.

          Makes about 2 cups

Butter Buds®

CURRIED LOW CAL DIP
(Low Calorie/Low Cholesterol)

4 packets BUTTER BUDS®
1 cup non-fat dry milk
8 tablespoons warm water
4 egg whites
1 teaspoon salt
2 tablespoons dry mustard
½ teaspoon SWEET 'N LOW® or
  equivalent sugar substitute
4 tablespoons vinegar
16 tablespoons oil
16 tablespoons hot water
8 teaspoons lemon juice
1 tablespoon curry powder (or, to
  taste)
1 tablespoon cayenne pepper (or,
  to taste)
"Dippers"*

Combine BUTTER BUDS,® dry milk,
water. In second bowl, beat egg
whites till foamy. Blend in salt,
mustard, sugar substitute and
vinegar. While beating, slowly add
oil, then contents of first bowl. Stir
thoroughly, then stir in hot water,
lemon juice and curry powder and
cayenne pepper as desired.

Makes about 4 cups

Calories: 35 (per ½ oz.)
Cholesterol: .18 mg.

*"DIPPERS"

1 2-pound flank steak
1 pound fresh mushrooms
1 pound string beans
1 large broccoli
1 large cauliflower

Brush steak with vegetable oil,
sprinkle with salt and pepper and
broil. Cut into very thin strips.
Steam string beans, broccoli and
cauliflower five minutes. Serve
mushrooms raw. Arrange on
serving platter surrounding bowl of
curried dip. Use fondue forks for
spearing and dipping.

ZURICH DIP

1 pkg. (8 oz.) cream cheese
1 pkg. (8 oz.) sour cream
1 tsp. instant minced onion
⅛ tsp. garlic powder
**1 can (3 oz.) OSCAR MAYER Real
   Bacon Bits**
Paprika

Combine cream cheese, sour
cream, onion and garlic; blend
well. Stir in bacon bits, reserving
some for garnish. Spoon into
shallow 1-quart glass casserole.

continued

continued

Bake in 350°F oven for 20 min.*
Sprinkle with paprika and reserved
bacon bits. Serve warm with fresh
vegetables and crackers.

Makes 2 cups

***Microwave** 5 min., stirring once,
halfway through heating. Stir;
garnish as above.

GARDEN VARIETY DIP
(Low Sodium/Low Calorie)

1½ cups plain yogurt
½ cup finely chopped PLANTERS®
  Dry Roasted Unsalted Peanuts
¼ cup minced fresh parsley
¼ cup finely chopped, peeled and
  seeded cucumber
2 tablespoons chopped green
  onion
¼ teaspoon dill weed
⅛ teaspoon ground white pepper

Thoroughly combine yogurt,
PLANTERS® Dry Roasted
Unsalted Peanuts, parsley,
cucumber, onion, dill weed and
white pepper. Chill 2 to 3 hours.

Serve with assorted fresh
vegetables such as carrots, celery,
cauliflower, mushrooms or
broccoli.   *Makes 2 cups*

Per tablespoon: 25 calories, 6 mg.
sodium

HOT CHILI-CHEESE DIP

1 15-oz. can ARMOUR® STAR
  Chili without Beans
1 4-oz. can chopped green chilies
1 lb. process American cheese,
  shredded
1 tablespoon Worcestershire sauce
Corn chips

Combine all ingredients, except
chips; heat, stirring occasionally,
over low heat until cheese melts.
Serve as a dip with corn chips.

4 cups

Microwave instructions: Combine
all ingredients, except chips, in
1½-qt. casserole. Cook, covered, 6
minutes, stirring occasionally.
Serve as a dip with corn chips.

TUNA DUNK
(Low Calorie/Low Cholesterol)

1 can (8 oz.) PET® Imitation Sour
  Cream
1 can (7 oz.) tuna, water-packed
  (drained and flaked)

continued

1 can (4 oz.) mushroom pieces
   and stems, drained and chopped
2 teaspoons instant minced onions
1 teaspoon Worcestershire sauce
1 tablespoon Sauterne (optional)

Mix all ingredients thoroughly in a
medium saucepan or chafing dish.
Heat until steaming. Serve warm
with crackers, potato chips,
pretzels, or French bread.

Makes about 2 cups

OLD EL PASO®
GUACAMOLE

2 large ripe avocados, peeled,
   pitted and sliced
1 jar (8 oz.) OLD EL PASO®
   Taco Sauce
½ cup chopped onion
2 tablespoons lemon or lime juice
1 teaspoon salt
½ teaspoon garlic powder
1 box (7 ½ oz.) OLD EL PASO®
   NACHIPS Tortilla Chips

Blend avocado slices, taco sauce,
onion, juice, salt and garlic powder
in blender or food processor. Chill.
Serve with NACHIPS.

Wyler's®

ORIENTAL DIP

1 cup mayonnaise or salad
  dressing
1 (8-ounce) container sour cream
1 (8-ounce) can water chestnuts,
  drained and finely chopped
2 tablespoons chopped pimiento
1 tablespoon sliced or chopped
  green onion
2 teaspoons WYLER'S® Beef-
  Flavor Instant Bouillon
½ teaspoon Worcestershire sauce
¼ teaspoon garlic powder
Potato chips or fresh vegetables

In medium bowl, combine all
ingredients except potato chips;
mix well. Cover; chill. Stir before
serving. Serve with chips.
Refrigerate leftovers.

Makes 2½ cups

KILBIRNIE CLAM DIP

1 can (7½ oz.) minced clams,
  undrained
⅓ cup JOHNNIE WALKER Red
8 oz. cream cheese, softened
1 envelope onion soup mix
1 cup sour cream

continued

continued

Combine clams with remaining ingredients; mix well. Chill. Serve with potato or corn chips, or crackers. *About 2½ cups*

ZESTY BEAN DIP

1 can (15 oz.) S&W Chili Beans, undrained
¼ tsp. chili powder (or more if desired)
1 can (4½ oz.) deviled ham
3 Tbsp. S&W Sweet Relish

Blend all ingredients till smooth in electric blender or mixer. To taste, add crumbled bacon bits, chopped onion or S&W Pimiento Slices, chopped. *Yield: 2 cups*

VARIATIONS:

Blend with medium size ripe avocado, or with a can (2 oz.) S&W Peeled Chili Peppers—or, blend in both.

VEGETABLE DIP
(Low Calorie/Low Cholesterol)

1 can (8 oz.) PET® Imitation Sour Cream
2 teaspoons instant minced onion
½ teaspoon garlic salt
¼ cup minced radishes
¼ cup minced green pepper
3 drops hot sauce

Combine all ingredients. Chill to blend the flavors. Serve with crackers, chips, or fresh crisp vegetables.

Makes about 1¼ cups dip

SAVORY YOGURT DIP
(Low Calorie)

1 packet HERB-OX Instant Onion
   Broth and Seasoning
1 cup plain yogurt
1½ tablespoons dried chopped
   chives
1½ tablespoons dried parsley

Combine all ingredients, mix well. Serve as a dip with raw celery, carrots, cauliflowerets, radishes, cucumber slices. Or use as a dressing for vegetable salads.

SNAPPY BEAN DIP

1 10-ounce can tomatoes and
   green chilies
1 pound sharp American cheese,
   grated
1 10½-ounce can FRITOS® Brand
   Jalapeño Bean Dip

continued

continued

Heat tomatoes and chilies with the cheese until cheese is melted. Add FRITOS® Brand Jalapeño Bean Dip and mix well. Serve hot with FRITOS® Brand Corn Chips, DORITOS® Brand Tortilla Chips, and RUFFLES® Brand Potato Chips.

KIWIFRUIT WINE CREAM DIP

¾ cup GIBSON Kiwifruit Wine
¼ teaspoon grated lemon rind
1 tablespoon cornstarch
¼ cup sugar
1 carton (9 oz.) of prepared whipped cream

Combine all ingredients except whipped cream in a saucepan. Cook and stir over high heat to a rolling boil; continue cooking mixture until it thickens. Cool mixture slightly; fold in whipped cream. Cover and chill 2 hours.

Makes approximately 2½ cups

Tip: Chill and serve as a dip with fruit kabobs, sliced pound cake, or gingersnaps.

Party Snacks

COFFEE GLAZED PECANS

1½ cups pecans
¼ cup sugar
2 measuring tablespoons water
2 measuring teaspoons TASTER'S
   CHOICE Instant Freeze-Dried
   Coffee
¼ measuring teaspoon cinnamon

In large skillet or electric skillet*,
combine pecans, sugar, water,
TASTER'S CHOICE and cinnamon;
bring to a boil over medium heat,
stirring constantly. Boil 3 minutes,
stirring constantly until pecans are
well glazed. Spread on waxed
paper to cool.
   Makes: 1½ cups glazed pecans

*NOTE: In electric skillet, heat all
         ingredients approximately
         4 minutes at 225°F.
         stirring constantly.

ROASTED PARTY PECANS

Toss 1 cup unsalted pecan halves
in 1 tablespoon olive or salad

continued

continued

oil mixed with 1 tablespoon Worcestershire sauce. Roast in shallow baking pan in slow oven (275°) for 30 minutes, stirring often. Drain on paper towel; sprinkle with salt.

VARIATION:

For a less spicy taste, place 1 pound of pecan halves in baking pan with ½ stick of butter or margarine. Bake at 225° for 30 to 45 minutes, stirring frequently. Spread on wax paper and salt to taste.

Favorite recipe from National Pecan Marketing Council

ORIENTAL ALMONDS

1½ tablespoons butter or
   margarine
1½ tablespoons Worcestershire
   sauce
1 teaspoon salt
¼ teaspoon cinnamon
⅛ teaspoon chili powder
Dash hot pepper sauce
1 package (10 ounces) BLUE
   DIAMOND® Blanched Whole
   Almonds (2 cups)

Melt butter in two-quart baking dish in a 300 degree F. oven. Stir in Worcestershire sauce, salt, cinnamon, chili powder and hot pepper sauce. Add almonds; stir until completely coated. Bake, stirring occasionally, 15 minutes or until almonds are crisp.

Makes 2 cups

NABISCO
BRANDS INC

BARBECUE RANCHO SNACKS
(Low Calorie)

¼ cup butter or margarine
3 tablespoons barbecue sauce
¾ teaspoon garlic salt
¼ teaspoon barbecue spice
4 cups NABISCO® SPOON SIZE
  Shredded Wheat

Melt butter or margarine in a 13 × 9 × 2-inch baking pan. Blend in next three ingredients. Add SPOON SIZE Shredded Wheat. Cook and stir gently until cereal is well coated. Bake in a preheated moderate oven (350°F.) 15 to 18 minutes or until lightly browned and crisp. Cool. *Makes 4 cups*

About 6 calories per Barbecue Rancho Snack

SCRIMMAGE

½ cup butter or margarine
4 cups NABISCO® SPOON SIZE
   Shredded Wheat
1 cup mixed nuts
¼ cup granulated sugar
1½ teaspoons ground cinnamon
½ cup DROMEDARY Chopped
   Dates

In large skillet melt butter or
margarine. Stir in next two
ingredients; sauté over medium
heat until toasted, shaking skillet
occasionally. Combine sugar and
cinnamon. Toss with cereal
mixture and dates; let cool.
                Makes about 5½ cups

PEANUT BUTTER PARTY MIX

2 tablespoons MAZOLA®/NUCOA®
   Margarine
⅓ cup SKIPPY® Creamy Peanut
   Butter
2 cups bite-size toasted wheat
   biscuits
2 cups bite-size toasted rice
   biscuits
¼ cup dry-roasted peanuts

In large skillet melt margarine over
low heat. Stir in peanut butter until
thoroughly mixed. Toss cereal and
nuts in mixture until coated.
Remove from heat. Spread on
ungreased cookie sheet. Bake in
375°F oven 8 minutes or until
golden brown. Drain on paper
towels.   *Makes about 4 cups*

Morton Salt

HOMEMADE TORTILLA CHIPS

3 cups flour
1 cup yellow cornmeal
4 teaspoons baking powder
1 tablespoon shortening
1 egg, beaten
1 cup water
Oil
MORTON Popcorn Salt

*Up to 1 Week or Day Before
Serving:* In large bowl, mix flour,
cornmeal, and baking powder. Mix
in shortening with fork. Stir in egg
and water to form a stiff dough.
Knead 5 minutes. Divide into 4
parts. Roll each into a 10-inch
square, about ⅛-inch thick; cut into

continued

continued

2-inch squares. Divide each square
into 2 triangles. Fry in 1-inch hot
oil (about 360°F.) about 2 minutes,
or until golden on both sides. Drain
on paper towels. Sprinkle with
popcorn salt. Cool. Store in airtight
containers or plastic bags.

Just Before Serving: Place tortilla
chips in lined basket or on
decorative plate.

Makes about 1½ pounds or
200 chips

QUAKER

SUPER SNACK CRUNCH

- **½ cup butter or margarine**
- **⅓ cup sugar**
- **⅓ cup strawberry or apricot**
  preserves
- **2 cups QUAKER® Oats (Quick or**
  Old Fashioned, uncooked)
- **¾ cup coarsely chopped nuts**
- **1 cup raisins or chopped dates**

Heat oven to 325°F. In large
saucepan, combine butter, sugar
and preserves. Cook over low heat,
stirring constantly, until well
blended and smooth; remove from
heat. Add oats and nuts; mix until

dry ingredients are thoroughly coated. Spread mixture evenly into ungreased 13 × 9-inch baking pan. Bake for 35 to 40 minutes or until golden brown, stirring occasionally. Add raisins; mix well. Spread mixture onto ungreased cookie sheet or aluminum foil; cool. Store in tightly covered container in cool dry place or refrigerator.

Makes about 6 cups

VARIATION:

Omit raisins or chopped dates.

CEREAL SCRAMBLE

¼ cup butter or margarine
2 tablespoons light brown sugar, firmly packed
¾ teaspoon ground cinnamon
2 cups NABISCO® SPOON SIZE Shredded Wheat
2 cups coarsely crushed TEAM Flakes Cereal
1 cup DROMEDARY Chopped Dates
¼ cup chopped salted peanuts
Milk, optional

Melt butter or margarine in large skillet; blend in brown sugar and cinnamon. Add next four ingredients and toss over low heat

continued

continued

until well coated. Cool to room
temperature. Store in airtight
container in refrigerator. Serve with
milk, if desired.

Makes about 5½ cups

**Ralston Purina
Company**

TRADITIONAL CHEX® PARTY MIX

½ cup butter or margarine
1¼ teaspoons seasoned salt
4½ teaspoons Worcestershire
  sauce
2 cups CORN CHEX® Cereal
2 cups RICE CHEX® Cereal
2 cups BRAN CHEX® Cereal
2 cups WHEAT CHEX® Cereal
1 cup salted mixed nuts

Preheat oven to 250°. Heat butter
in large shallow roasting pan
(about 15 × 10 × 2-inches) in oven
until melted. Remove. Stir in
seasoned salt and Worcestershire
sauce. Add CHEX® and nuts. Mix
until all pieces are coated. Heat in
oven 1 hour. Stir every 15 minutes.
Spread on absorbent paper to cool.

Makes about 9 cups

GOLD'N NUT CRUNCH!

1 can (12 ounces) FISHER®
   Mixed Nuts or 1 jar (12 ounces)
   FISHER® Dry Roasted Peanuts
¼ cup LAND O LAKES® Sweet
   Cream Butter, melted
¼ cup grated parmesan cheese
¼ teaspoon garlic powder
¼ teaspoon ground oregano
¼ teaspoon celery salt
4 cups GOLDEN GRAHAMS®
   Cereal

Heat oven to 300°. Mix nuts and butter in medium bowl until well coated. Add cheese, garlic powder, oregano and celery salt; toss until well coated. Spread in ungreased jelly roll pan, 15½ × 10½ × 1 inch. Bake, stirring occasionally, 15 minutes. Stir in cereal; cool. Store in airtight container.

About 6½ cups snack

Skillet Method: Heat butter in heavy 10-inch skillet until melted. Add remaining ingredients; stir until well coated. Heat over low heat, stirring occasionally, 5 minutes; cool.

NATURAL MUNCH

2½ quarts popped POPEYE
Popcorn (about ⅓ cup
unpopped)
1 cup salted peanuts
1 cup wheat germ
1 cup sugar
⅓ cup honey
⅓ cup water
¼ cup butter or margarine, melted
½ teaspoon salt

Preheat oven to 250°F. Grease two
15 × 10 × 1-inch jelly-roll pans. In a
large greased bowl toss together
popcorn, peanuts, and wheat germ.
Set aside. Combine remaining
ingredients in 2-quart saucepan.
Cook over medium heat, stirring
constantly until sugar is dissolved
and mixture begins to boil.
Continue cooking until mixture
reaches 250°F. on candy
thermometer (hard ball stage). Pour
over popcorn mixture slowly,
stirring to coat. Spread in prepared
jelly-roll pans. Bake 45 minutes,
stirring every 10 or 15 minutes.
Remove from oven; stir to
distribute flavor. When cool, store
in tightly covered containers.

3 quarts

MAYPO® GRANOLA MIX

1 box 14 oz. MAYPO® 30-Second
   Oatmeal
1 cup WHEATENA®
¾ cup brown sugar, firmly packed
1 teaspoon salt
⅓ cup instant non-fat dry milk
   (optional)
½ cup oil
½ cup water
½ cup *each:* sesame seeds, small
   sunflower seeds, finely chopped
   nuts
¾ cup shredded coconut
½ cup raisins or dates, finely
   chopped

In a large bowl, mix MAYPO®
WHEATENA® brown sugar, salt and
dry milk. Combine oil and water;
add to cereal mixture and stir only
until mixed. Add the sesame
seeds, sunflower seeds, nuts,
coconut and fruit; stir only until
mixed. Spread mixture on large
cookie sheet (or use four 9-inch pie
pans). Bake in preheated 250°F.
oven for 1 hour, stirring mixture
about every 15 minutes to brown
evenly. Remove from oven; cool;
store in air-tight container.

Makes about 2¼ pounds
(eight 1 cup servings)

Acknowledgments

The Editors of CONSUMER GUIDE® wish to thank the companies and organizations listed for use of their recipes and artwork. For further information contact the following:

Amber Brand Deviled Smithfield Ham, *see* Smithfield Ham

Armour and Co.
Phoenix, AZ 85077

Arnold Sorensin, Inc.
401 Hackensack Ave.
Hackensack, NJ 07601

Atalanta Corp.
17 Varick St.
New York, NY 10013

Austin, Nichols & Co., Inc.
1290 Ave. of the Americas
New York, NY 10019

Baltimore Spice Co., The
Baltimore, MD 21208

Banquet Foods Corp.
Ballwin, MO 63011

Bertolli USA
So. San Francisco, CA 94080

Best Foods
Englewood Cliffs, NJ 07632

Blue Diamond®
P.O. Box 1768
Sacramento, CA 95808

Booth Fisheries Corp.
2 N. Riverside Plaza
Chicago, IL 60606

Borden Inc.
Columbus, OH 43215

Breyers® Yogurt, *see* Kraft, Inc. Dairy Group

Bumble Bee®, *see* Castle & Cooke

Butter Buds®, *see* Cumberland Packing

Butterball® Turkey, *see* Swift

Calavo Growers of California
Box 3486 Terminal Annex
Los Angeles, CA 90051

California Table Grape Commission,
see Pacific Kitchen

Campbell Soup Co.
Camden, NJ 08101

Castle & Cooke Foods
San Francisco, CA 94119

Cheez-It®, *see* Sunshine Biscuits

Cheez-Ola®, *see* Fisher Cheese

Chex® Cereals, *see* Ralston Purina

The Christian Brothers®
655 Beach St.
San Francisco, CA 94109

Claussen, *see* Oscar Mayer

Coca-Cola Co.
Houston, TX 77001

Coco Casa™, *see* Holland House

Cookin' Good® Chicken
Showell Farms, Inc.
Showell, MD 21862

Corn Diggers Snack, *see* Nabisco

Cracker Barrel, *see* Kraft, Inc.

Cumberland Packing Corp.
2 Cumberland St.
Brooklyn, NY 11205

Dannon Co., Inc., The
Long Island City, NY 11101

Del Monte Corp.
P.O. Box 3575
San Francisco, CA 94119

Denmark Cheese Association
4415 W. Harrison St.
Hillside, IL 60162

Dromedary, *see* Nabisco

Dubonnet, *see* Schenley

Durkee Foods
Strongsville, OH 44136

Eckrich, Peter, & Sons, Inc.
Ft. Wayne, IN 46801

Finlandia Swiss Cheese, *see* Atalanta

Fisher Cheese Co.
Wapakoneta, OH 45895

Fisher Nut Co.
P.O. Box 43434
St. Paul, MN 55164

Fleischmann's®, *see* Standard Brands

French, R.T., Co., The
Rochester, NY 14692

Frito-Lay, Inc.
P.O. Box 35034
Dallas, TX 75235

Gerber Products Co.
Fremont, MI 49412

Gibson Wine Co.
Elk Grove, CA 95624

Green Giant®, *see* Pillsbury

Heinz U.S.A.
Pittsburgh, PA 15230

Hi Ho® Crackers, *see* Sunshine Biscuits

High Sea, *see* Robinson Canning

Hillshire Farm®
New London, WI 54961

Holland House Brands Co.
Ridgefield, NJ 07657

Hunt-Wesson Kitchens
Fullerton, CA 92634

Imperial Sugar Co.
Sugar Land, TX 77478

Iroquois Grocery Products, Inc.
111 High Ridge Rd.
Stamford, CT 06905

Jacquin, Charles, et Cie, Inc.
2633 Trenton Ave.
Philadelphia, PA 19125

Jays Foods, Inc.
825 E. 99th St.
Chicago, IL 60628

Jimmy Dean® Companies
1341 W. Mockingbird Ln.
Dallas, TX 75247

Johnnie Walker Red, *see* Somerset
Importers

Kikkoman International Inc.
P.O. Box 784
San Francisco, CA 94111

King Oscar Fine Foods
Millburn, NJ 07041

Kraft, Inc.
Glenview, IL 60025

Kraft, Inc. Dairy Group
Philadelphia, PA 19101

Land O'Lakes, Inc.
P.O. Box 116
Minneapolis, MN 55440

Lea & Perrins, Inc.
Fair Lawn, NJ 07410

Lindsay International Inc.
Visalia, CA 93277

Lipton, Thomas J., Inc.
Englewood Cliffs, NJ 07632

Liquore Galliano®, *see* "21" Brands

Louisiana Brand, *see* Robinson
Canning

Maypo®, *see* Standard Milling

Mazola®/Nucoa®, *see* Best Foods

Minute Maid®, *see* Coca-Cola

Morton Salt
110 N. Wacker Dr.
Chicago, IL 60606

Nabisco, Inc.
East Hanover, NJ 07936

Nalley's Fine Foods Div.
3303 S. 35th
Tacoma, WA 98411

National Pecan Marketing Council
1800 Peachtree Rd., N.W.
Atlanta, GA 30309

Nestlé Co., Inc.
100 Bloomingdale Rd.
White Plains, NY 10605

Northwest Cherry Growers, *see* Pacific
Kitchen

Old El Paso®, *see* Pet

Oscar Mayer & Co.
Madison, WI 53707

Pacific Bartlett Growers, Inc., *see*
Pacific Kitchen

Pacific Kitchen
300 Elliott Ave., W., Suite 250
Seattle, WA 98119

Parkay, *see* Kraft, Inc.

Pepperidge Farm, Inc.
Norwalk, CT 06856

Pernod, *see* Austin, Nichols

Pet Inc.
St. Louis, MO 63166

Philadelphia Brand Cream Cheese, *see* Kraft, Inc.

Pillsbury Co., The
608 Second Ave., S.
Minneapolis, MN 55402

Planters®, *see* Standard Brands

Popeye, *see* Stokely-Van Camp

Premium Saltine Crackers, *see* Nabisco

Quaker Oats Co., The
Merchandise Mart Plaza
Chicago, IL 60654

Ralston Purina Co.
Checkerboard Square
St. Louis, MO 63188

Robinson Canning Co., Inc.
New Orleans, LA 70178

Romanoff® Caviar, *see* Iroquois

Schenley Affiliated Brands Corp.
888 Seventh Ave.
New York, NY 10106

Sealtest®, *see* Kraft Inc. Dairy Group

Sizzlean®, *see* Swift

Skippy® Peanut Butter, *see* Best Foods

Smithfield Ham & Products Co., Inc.
Smithfield, VA 23430

Snack Mate, *see* Nabisco

Somerset Importers, Ltd.
1114 Ave. of the Americas
New York, NY 10036

Standard Brands, Inc.
625 Madison Ave.
New York, NY 10022

Standard Milling Co.
P.O. Box 410
Kansas City, MO 64141

Stock, *see* Schenley

Stokely-Van Camp, Inc.
941 N. Meridian St.
Indianapolis, IN 46206

Sunshine Biscuits, Inc.
245 Park Ave.
New York, NY 10017

Swanson, *see* Campbell Soup

Sweet 'N Low®, *see* Cumberland Packing

Swift & Co.
Oak Brook, IL 60521

Tabasco®
McIlhenny Co.
Milford, TX 76670

Taster's Choice, *see* Nestlé

Team Flakes, *see* Nabisco

Treasure Cave® Blue Cheese, *see* Swift

"21" Brands, Inc.
75 Rockefeller Plaza
New York, NY 10019

Underwood, Wm., Co.
Westwood, MA 02090

Valio Gruyere Cheese, *see* Atalanta

Velveeta, *see* Kraft, Inc.

Virginia Dare Extract Co., Inc.
882 Third Ave.
Brooklyn, NY 11232

Wheatena®, *see* Standard Milling

Wild Turkey, *see* Austin, Nichols

Wispride Cheese Food, *see* Nestlé

Wolff's® Kasha
The Birkett Mills
Penn Yan, NY 14527

Wright, E.H., Co., Inc.
783 Old Hickory Blvd.
Brentwood, TN 37027

Wyler's®, *see* Borden

Index